Notes of Light and Dark

Also from Dos Gatos Press

Wingbeats: Exercises and Practice in Poetry

Wingbeats II: Exercises and Practice in Poetry

Unknotting the Line: The Poetry in Prose

22 Poems & a Prayer for El Paso

Weaving the Terrain: 100-Word Southwestern Poems

Bearing the Mask: Southwestern Persona Poems

Lifting the Sky: Southwestern Haiku & Haiga

Shallow-Rooted Heart, Poems by Gregory Louis Candela

Circumference of Light, Poems by Bruce Noll

Letting Myself In, Poems by Anne McCrady

Redefining Beauty, Poems by karla k. morton

Notes of Light and Dark:
Southwestern Aubades and Nocturnes

Poetry of the Southwestern United States

Number 6

Scott Wiggerman and
David Meischen, Editors

Dos Gatos Press

Albuquerque, New Mexico

Notes of Light and Dark:
Southwestern Aubades and Nocturnes

© 2025, Dos Gatos Press
ISBN-13: 978-0-9973966-7-6

Notes of Light and Dark is the sixth in a series from Dos Gatos Press: Poetry of the Southwestern United States.

First Edition

Interior & Cover Design: David Meischen & Scott Wiggerman

Cover Art and Internal Images: from *As Above, So Below,*
a copper plate etching by Scott Wiggerman

Dos Gatos Press
6452 Kola Ct. NW
Albuquerque, NM 87120
www.dosgatospress.org

in memory of

Gary Worth Moody

November 13, 1951 – March 18, 2025

Quintessential Southwestern poet—
a kind and giving member
of the New Mexico poetry community

I wanted to write a poem
to equal the sky, starlight
and moon shadow giving way
to frosted sun.

Michael McIrvin

On Brown Mountain

We came to walk a desert trail
and dawdled like we often do,
day heat gone to evening shiver,
darkening rocks and unseen turns,
cactus armed and looking dangerous.

Downhill a crow's dark humor,
road and car still a mile away.
Am I afraid of losing the way?
Wasn't I hungry for a dose of desert.
a quest for quietude?

And now you complain
it feels as if we've been dropped into an apocalypse,
this blooming nightmare
of saguaro blossoms smelling like melons and rotten socks.

Maybe you're afraid, too, of getting lost again,
like when our lives seemed darkly thorny,
barren of what we couldn't say or do,
our marriage-on-the-rocks
with no clear markers to find the way.

But that was then and this is no déjà vu.
Like some poet said
we can bury that burden-bundle under a rock
and if we need to howl we should howl,
grab a mouthful of moonlight and stars.

Pamela Ahlen

The first time I went out in the desert

It felt right standing tall on a ledge of rock,
my arms opened wide to embrace
a new morning creeping in all pink to rose
to gold, casting light on me, inside of me,
rising out of me and into what seemed
an infinity of sand and sky.
I felt empowered, yet of no importance,
miniscule, no need to hide
behind my usual armor of thorns,
lizard silent,
wind silent,
rabbit and cactus still asleep,
no javelina roaming the dry creek bed,
not one cloud to shed one tear . . .

Pamela Ahlen

hunt

i rattle the truck across the last cattleguard before dropping down into lower lost canyon, rifle across my lap, emptied now of shells. the 345 kilovolt powerline's steel lattice silhouetted black against a cloudless and dying sky, the cables tailing off symmetrically in both directions. the skyline a reddish-pink farewell to the colding sun, blanketed by a strange yellow-green ambiguity held down firmly and progressively by the dust blue-black of the encroaching night. the sun sinks at goodman point; sleeping ute mountain floats on the horizon just to the south.

i climb past walker's sawmill, traverse the highway, and coast the last mile to the house. my mind, prodded by the beer, moves back to a late night in july, when this hunt really began. coming home late from work, close to eleven, i see eyes in the far corner of the property. i go past the driveway and swerve the headlights into the pasture of snakeweed and prairie dog holes: seven bucks. eyes like murky green planets, liquid in their skulls. antlers connected by diaphanous lines to brilliant, penetrating stars, pulled out and upward in graceful, hauntingly delicate ways, now, and far into the past, far into the future. ghosts that live inside me until i can hunt, fueling that archaic and unrelenting desire.

Luther Allen

again, for the first time

perfectly drunk
in perfect company

on edge of ruins canyon
a spray of piñon, juniper
near sunset
moonrise to come

thinking
for 100,000 years
no—
i cannot understand
that time span—
for 10,000 years
    yes, every evening
    of each day
    of my life
that long   that many

every evening the same
crickets
toads
doves
shrinking light
the same

a lunar sliver, the leading edge
just to the north
of ute peak
at bottom
of attenuated spring
cumulonimbus

every evening
different
drink everything
then

O!
huge and bulbous
quavering
moon—

winged moon!

       Luther Allen

driving into the night

into cortez at one a.m.
to pick up a special order
off the trailways bus

the radio, otherworldly at this hour
disorients, transmogrifying this familiar route
into a vast strangeness, a dream

    i remember the last
    time i was up this late—
    san juan arm of lake powell
    catfishing with will
    steve and ron
    motor running, headlights
    on to see the pole tips
                    no fish
    driving back to kayenta
    will, who is somewhere between 50 & 70,
    at the wheel, beer in hand
    i'm so sleepy, so tired
    so fretted with the black road, the speed
        i finally give up to
        the wide desert air, the lonely radio
        the whine of tires
        deciding if i die tonight
        to at least be at peace with the moment

i get the package
among the abandoned, the drunk
the night travelers
not yet at their destination

if there is a destination

i start back home
at steve fuller's turn

    three raccoons
    on the edge of the road

    with no thought of death
    or even destination

    half-crouched, peering
    into the headlights

    Luther Allen

Mourning Near Kanab

When we have gone the stone will stop singing.
~ W. S. Merwin, "April"

Tramp up Deer Spring Wash mid-morn
Ascend the ziggurat path up to Pottery Knoll
    through red dust sage-scent
        shrouding stair-step sandstone outcrops.

Vermilion we geologists proclaim—
        Rocks the color of old dense bloods.

And the stone does not sing at this hour
    only   earlier
when crisp dawn offers promise.

Toasted and muted we climb to the top. Even
the scorpions stay away.   The horse has the best of it.
Yep, Bally knows the way up. We been here many's the time.
The ranch caretaker, high on his quarter horse, so proud of that knoll. And we as
    scientists do—observe the dusty ruins of pit houses, slabbed scarlet stones
    upturned shattered huddled
Possibly a family unit here . . . and oh, might this be a kiva?
    note the pottery shards everywhere scattered   scarred   burned and broken.
Basketmaker II—note the distinctive black and white markings. Really quite impressive.

And our hypotheses are—
    powerful and publishable constructs pontificating
    on loss and devastation in this searing 2nd millennial world.
It was climate change or warfare or both or neither.

People will go quiet in days to come.
Cinnabar rocks will lose
nothing.

Elizabeth L. Ambos

Collared Lizard

When dawn light strikes
the front of the house,
the collared lizard
and I come out.
We're sun worshippers
from way back.
I round the corner
and there he is, vertical,
patrolling the stucco
like a toy dinosaur—
thick and sturdy,
with the black neckbands
of a revolutionary.
His push-ups relate
epic tales of his race—
warring, wooing,
rock climbing—
and now the thrill
of a new dominion—
the sills, the eaves,
the clay roof tiles.
The mercury heads
for triple digits.
I retreat inside
leaving him to ride
the heat wave.

Cynthia Anderson

Visitation

A desert kit fox comes to the glass door
and looks straight through to the inside.

There he sees a man and a woman
at the breakfast table.

Called by a dream, he has answered.

He stands still as they move closer.
His plumed tail. His dark, searching eyes.

Then, a quick jump to the stone wall,
a trot up the hill, and gone.

> hospice wish
> a final transplant
> to the spirit realm

Cynthia Anderson

A Desert Song

The stillness of the dawn awakens me. A sweet, refreshing fragrance fills the air of sun-baked sand and earth upon a brief and sudden rain which comes unbidden with an early morning chill. And she, my Aztec princess, sleeps and rests her head upon my breast. Her jet-black hair streams down upon a reddened cheek, and while she sleeps, the desert, through an open window can be heard to breathe. Upon its breath, the fragrance of the rare and radiant flowers summoned from a dry and dormant bed, still damp from blessed rain which comes and goes, fickle as the breezes from a chain of distant, snow-capped mountain peaks. And only those who listen with their hearts can hear the song the lonely, haunted desert sings.

Conrado Aragón

Night Bloomer

In Chagall's paintings, horses
bloom from chimneys, crows' wings

petal into a lady's hat, a bride
dances on air and somehow klezmer music buzzes

from the frames;
that is, I feel something mournful

in the celebratory, the night opening
like a mouth to release peonies and roosters.

This year again a plague of moths
reincarnates, papers the doors and windows with flurry,

the smell of wings singing against bulbs, a carpet of spent thoraxes.
Frightening and a little bit beautiful, this abundance,

this rush-hour confluence on windshields, moths
gushing through the smallest openings, an invasion

of breathing. Their wings are well worn rags everyone is waving
all the time. Nothing is more unreal

than the real. For instance, the dog the neighbors exiled
to the backyard where it cried all night into our ears,

fermenting dreams with the kind of dread that wakes you
tearful and filled with a despair so dry and bitter

you think you will never taste anything sweet again.
In the morning the yard is empty, as if such desperation

never existed, as if sorrow were an imaginary state and no one and nothing
was ever abandoned. I wander my own yard counting little storms

of lost feathers, a dozen holes where something has uprooted
all the newly planted seedlings, a huddle of wrens

scolding as I reach to pick the single strawberry
the night has cajoled into perfect ripeness.

Rebecca Aronson

Fireflies

In the field swarms of them
blink a galaxy into existence,
constellations that form and dissolve, gallop
above the unmown grasses, dandelions, prairie
coneflower, false parsley, the scent of impending rain
that rises like laughing gas from the soil; we laugh
and run a little in the uneven dark, wanting
to catch each bright golden light.
In the hand they are small
and plain, as easily unsettled
as the weakest of our ambitions.
We want to keep them
in jars, our own magical lanterns,
but they are not to be had, not to be
made any use of beyond the longing
they spark, light years later,
for a world in which it is enough
to have been once dazzled.

Rebecca Aronson

And now distant coyotes' voices
pierce the stillness, singing the sun up.

Victoria Stefani

Peace Signs under Van Gogh Skies

A delicate breeze blows
Van Gogh's starry vision
across late night moonlight,
Dodge tire imprints
crisscross red Okie dirt

Summer clouds swim
through smooth cobalt skies,
turning 10 p.m. to midnight
and 2 a.m. to an endless abyss

soft skin sings to me,

bare feet dangling from the edge
of rusted old bridge rafters,
a mysterious secret spot
shared by strangers
sharing secrets like old lovers,

two souls reflected
in silent still low river waters

Your peace sign tattoo,
pricked to some sacred
place that I somehow forget
through clouded memories,

but the imprint still stitched
to eyes ten years older,

still there, still clear
like the slow-moving river
and warm gentle winds
with just a hint
of October rolling in

Like the touch of soft skin,
softer lips
a shirt
with too many straps
and too much room to sin

Cody Baggerly

The Lawrence Tree, 1929

*The big pine tree in front of the house, standing still
and unconcerned and alive . . .*

~ D.H. Lawrence

O'Keeffe stretched out
On the narrow bench

Her face to the night
Saw the tree suspended

Held by stars

Great ponderosa
Guarding words

The artist speaks
In color & shape

The wind lives up there

Virginia Barrett

Burch Street, Taos

~ Jane Kenyon, "Three Songs at the End of Summer"

The crows' clamor brings me outside in time to catch
the sunset. I thank them, and while we don't speak
the same language, I believe they understand.

As their dark flapping fills the sky's dyeing, I say *sorry*
that the town cut down the dead pine where they often
perched, draped in somber capes: bleak and assertive.

Why do crows steal into so many poems?—as if
the Celtic goddess, the Morrigan, who could shapeshift
into the artful bird, intervenes.

I've never conjured wings, but I wore lots of black
living in San Francisco, where corvid-authority
is less than here, but rampant enough.

Crows and cloud colors gone now, cicadas take
over the coming-night sound: a steady hum—
like need, or the beat of a pueblo drum.

Virginia Barrett

Home

Middle of the night I think of them
floating high above us,
astronauts in the Space Station
moving round and round our planet.

Till the docking module arrives,
months from now, their tiny home in space
lacks even the comfort of gravity,
the smells of earth and leaves.

How I have longed for home
in the midst of travels,
to make it back to that gathering
of lights far below our circling aircraft,

then closer, closer as we come in
for a landing and finally touch down,
the ground rising up all around.
The terminal with its smells of coffee and tacos.

The taxi ride home, windows wide
to warm, humid air, soft
as a pair of old cotton p.j.'s on my skin.
"Turn here!" at the sight of the Ebbtide Lounge.

Another block uphill and we're there:
flat roofed house, maguey plants pointing skyward,
cedar elm, bur oak, Olivia, the neighborhood cat
hurrying to rub against our legs.

Slow, rhythmic throb of cicadas
in the welcoming darkness of home.

Patricia Spears Bigelow

Broken Moon

I like the way the moon
is mostly broken during the long nights
of winter. Puts itself back together
a piece at a time: white shining
against the dark, until it's whole as an egg
and then a perfect sphere of light
accompanied by companion stars or alone.
It soon begins to lose that roundness night by night.
Life exacts a heavy toll for shine.

During moonless times, we almost forget
its smile, its calming luminescence until
one night we see that shimmery sylph
perched on the branch of a prickly mesquite
like some exotic bird come home to roost
and we breathe a sigh as if an old friend
has returned from the grave
and survived to illumine our lives again.

Patricia Spears Bigelow

First Light

From the open window
a chaos of light filters
through the open weave
of linen curtains,
brings with its endless bright
wafts of soft blue sighs,
the cactus wren aubade,
and scent of Apache plume
lifting from the desert.
I am not yet ready to rise,
not yet ready to push
away the romance of dreams,
but invite morning
into the comfort of bed.

Elizabeth Black

Wintering

In my room overlooking the treetops, I see
the cardinal and his smaller mate
moving over leafless branches.
It wasn't for you I wanted to burn down
my life, but the idea of you, like a stick
of incense giving up its vanilla, its patchouli,
freezing something not meant
to be frozen. Minor blue-violet,
summer dusk. Outside a tree-of-heaven
tilts skyward, its acrid, awkward
blossoms, below the soil a monster
of inter-connected roots. To hold what
is fleeting next to what will last
or what refuses to be destroyed.
Tree-of-heaven also known as knotweed,
able to spring back from the slightest live
stalk. I don't know what to make
of such survival—when young it was
easy to see pain as merely a means
of pushing through, to believe in abundance.
I had a memory the other day of the dusty
vaulted ceiling of the narrow church
we used to visit, named for San Ysidro,
patron saint of farmers, rain prayers.
Being a gardener, he knows death
to his fingertips, the practice of planting,
planting, seeing nothing flower. And yet
tonight, two small red birds lift off from
the bare branches of the dying laurel,
follow each other all through the morning.

Sheila Black

A Sudden Thaw

Not the clamping down as when
a dog grips a bird in its jaws and shakes,
but the opposite—a crackling
under surface, gold gush
that wakes you one morning
to find the live oaks already in leaf,
a hard echo as when ice gives
way. And how to give up the bad
habits of the bad self.
That day we walked out into
ice storm—two frost-gloved trees
with two cardinals flitting between
—the scissoring motion of
their wings and how I kept
thinking *to cut the air,*
as if it were a thing I might do.
Not the rare voyage, but the morning
commute—the mess of March:
mud, dead leaves; yet overnight
the paper-thin petals of wild poppies
unfolding red, arterial.

Sheila Black

How We Live Now

He knows where the owls are. I don't until
he shows me, and when he does, we
witness the parents feeding the children,
going out to savage what they can,
and then the sweet motion of the tiny
feathered throats. We hold the binoculars
to our eyes as you might hold the words
of a familiar catechism. We recognize what
we see; yet cannot forget the curled blue
mouse bodies. The little owls' eyes shine,
not like the moon, but like the flickering.
neon signs along our local highway,
which shiver at such a rate they make
our city seem larger, stranger than it is.
Tell us how we must live, we ask the flat
disk of a moon we know will never answer.
The question still feels important. Another day,
another raptor—this time the caracara, two
together, hooded-eyed, perched on a telephone
pole above a cinderblock ranch where a gray
tabby has crept onto the lawn to die after being
hit by a car. The birds lift their wings—oh
span of great distance. *Here we are.*

Sheila Black

Tucson Spring

Here, we've nothing like the showy foxglove,
its tubular blooms of flamboyant Victorian-
crimson, blush-rose and frosted porcelain,
the flowers of caste gardens
with their indistinct honeyed scent.

Neither do we awaken to relish
a morning's seagull overture, the enigmatic
notes, drawn by plovers' prints
across fresh waved sand.

Nor are we blessed with clover's harlequin carpet,
the abundance of green a luscious lull over
even the most troubled minds.

But in this springless springtime morning,
the quail prance prim and plump as princes
with the knowledge of what not everyone
will slow to see:

this procession of budding, blossoming splendor,
beebrush with its horns of infinitesimal petals,
nopal flowering in lemon, salmon, and heliotrope,
the colors borrowed from sunrise, with petals
as delicate as the skin behind your knee,
Palo Verde igniting in glorious garden arrival,

and the ocotillo, veined and leafless,
gone dormant in this drought,
wielding, in its cracked limbs,
fistfuls of fire.

Gia Bloomstrand

A faint fragrance
hangs in the air—
ponderosa pine in the damp morning—
the last note of a song,
the brush stroke of watercolor
soaking into paper.

Vince Puzick

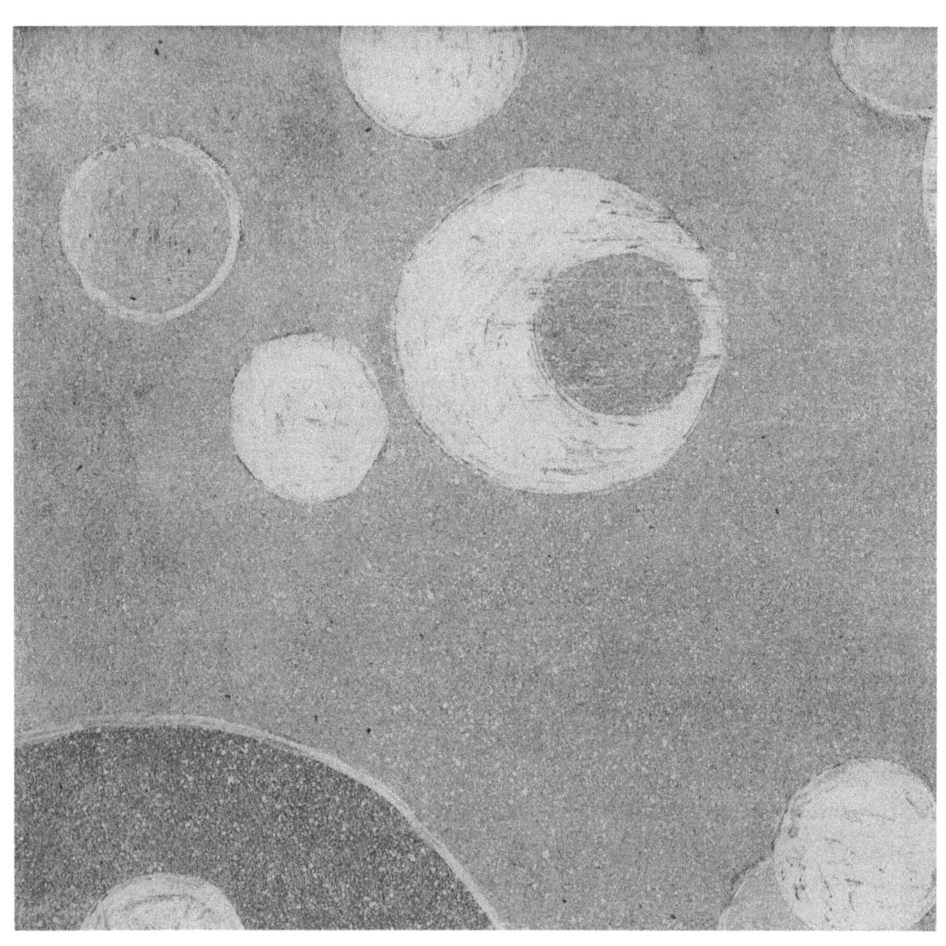

Cycles

My bike makes its first pass through the dark streets,
still lamp-lit, early, and empty of cars.
The air quickens with a nearly-dawn breeze.
The sky replies by erasing the stars.

As I set out, signs of life are quite sparse:
The houses wink open their window eyes.
I grip more tightly on my handle bars.
The night birds settle, as a crow cracks wise.

Folks stir in the houses with unshuttered eyes,
Light is beginning to charm the oak trees.
An owl's last hoot prompts a sparrow's replies.
I pedal hard, feel a throb in my knees.

By my second pass, light ignites the trees.
The birds are busy with paean and plaint.
Pedaling burns both my thighs and my knees.
Sun sparkles on casements as on fresh paint.

Blue jays greet the morning without restraint.
Their vocal practice begins in earnest.
Sun gives each bloom the dazzle of a saint.
Sprinklers shhhsh, eperanza is burnished;

Crepe myrtle, Pride of Barbados, furnish
The sun with more hues to highlight, release.
Even weeds by the road are refurbished.
I'm swamped by serenity, awed by peace.

My third pass. I cede my exclusive lease,
For others are claiming the day as well.
Bicyclists, joggers, dog walkers, increase.
To greet each, I thumb my bicycle bell.

But of this morning there's still more to tell:
arthritic gestures of two dying oaks,
the bike's cadence casting a hazy spell,
the whisper of gravel on the wheels' spokes.

Then my trance ends. Just now I provoke
Three white-tailed does and a dappled fawn.
At a rare moment when no other folk
Could see them cropping on this neighbor's lawn.

They return my glance with surprise, then—gone.
The wind has decamped. A day without breeze,
But one with four deer on a neighbor's lawn.
My bike makes its last pass through the bright streets.

Christine H. Boldt

San Bernardino After the War

I grew up in the desert in a one-story
baby blue rambler with white scalloped eaves
and a penchant for cozying up
to its neighbors and chatting long into the night.

The circle of homes nodded and smiled
as children poured in and out
of windows and doors, rambling in waves
from kitchen to kitchen for Kool-Aid and crackers
and marbles and jacks, rolling onto lawns,
linking hands to call out *red rover red rover*
why don't you come over.

When the sun slipped away for a good night's rest,
children planted themselves like small round beans
in drowsy beds under plump cotton quilts
singing *all the pretty horses,* and dreaming
of copper bays to ride them away
on tumbleweed trails, out to the soft brown hills
under the sun-warped sky.

   Sharon V. Brown

Evening Altar

My barely blue communion plate is filled with yellow ash
orange cottonwood leaves and one red button
to welcome evening and fall of this year

At twilight its candlelight mimics
the waning light of late summer days
and paler skies

I will keep it company until
a harvest moon helps collect
my thoughts on a yet unequal night

The open door of my casita invites
wind chimes in to share
mooncakes and sage tea
in expectation of nightfall
when I gently press my finger
upon that always red reset button

Kathleen Burke

The Rust Red Hills

after a Georgia Keeffe painting by the same title

It is not rust-red hills, hyphenated,
one, nor a churning of red to orange,
nor an inadvertent sequence of naming,
a clarification of red
or a state of red's dying by oxidation,
but rust as its own condition, prominence,

rust, a softened appearance of early evening,
not a sunset's red glare, a lonely color,
as she was lonely,
the gloss on her lips
puffed after kissing
long gone, her partner
more the dry hills
than the moist body of husband
two thousand miles removed.

She could not choose a color of green.
Earth and she were not verdant, naïve,
and the thrust of birth
and human population's endurance
she could not trick from eye to brushstroke.

She sat with a rust laid bare by time,
a rust that had entered her,
filled her brushstrokes
with those deep, cleft hills
rounded like flesh
love could no longer provide.

Jeff Burt

Canyon Moon

They are full, these candles, filling the one long
room of my cabin, gathering their eyes from the
moon that rolls silently up the orchard past trees
spreading with new pears and apples. Leaves ripple
from white light—not evening air, not night weather.

This same singing swath of light fuels cicadas, shoots owls
off on desperate pathways littered with new dead,
stops poorwills from long calling, makes the
canyon's lone black bear pause, look up, tongue
the air for a taste of whiteness.

Above the moving canopy of apples, stars from all
directions retreat handing light to the moon—their
one consistent teacher. The moon pours like an
offering through the cabin's window,

stalks the orchard like a cool magnet making grass
and apple trees leap up, apple roots and old metals
rise. Under its light, the canyon trembles:

a huge, clothed feeling stirring, ready to break
and soar.

Michael Burwell

The Moon is Not My Mother

The moon is no door, no eye, no dream vacation destination.
The moon is not my mother, who hovers instead in her near-boneless
state like a moth, impelled by the smell of her roommate's dank musk
or the ruffles that frill at the sill. Sometimes she calls me mommy
and opens her arms, girl again, missing for years, returned to the dusty home
of aprons, pots seething on the stove. The moon is no fortune teller, no
epiphany. Not the lamp I light when I shake out her sheets full of crumbs.
When we bathed her those long days of the plague, she moaned in pleasure.
We scrubbed and scrubbed her mottled back, half wrapped in plastic to protect
her wounds. Separate moons, we had never touched much. Instead, we tended
boys like trees in Colorado soil—pruned and clipped, mulch-fed and watered.
Those boys played war in the iris-clad ditches. The moon is no witness, no revelation.
Once I dreamt the moon fell to earth, and in that moon, a door, and from that door,
flew moths. Or maybe mothers, I thought, back for the bones they were missing.

Tina Carlson

Santa Fe River, No King's Day, 2025

At dawn, the scaled quail pierces air with her single notes
and flycatchers echo across this intermittent river
while swallows swoop and plunge, like warplanes,
over what is left of water. Soon this bed will be dry:
stone and trash, prints in the sand. Citizens
on the banks: cottonwood, fescue, coyote willow,
bend slightly in a breeze. A snake unfurls her thin
flag of stripes, then heads for shade. When this morning's
urgent songs of hunger and mating subside, we will
march to the plaza, calling out into the warming air.
Brush fires burned in the night, and today will be hotter
than most: crowds of sound switched up with dissent,
a plunder of tanks. We linger awhile in the aviary
of this still early day. Fledglings practice flight.

Tina Carlson

Gary in Flight

Early morning he sits, feathered and wet, hunkered
in river's round stones. Later he perches outside
and peers in, a poem behind the glass. He eats
a sparrow plucked from its nest. I like to imagine
my dead friend as raptor—how he used to capture
then tether those hawks, and they flew from his wrist
to learn limits. Now he is everywhere: river-bird threat,
high tree caller. Raucous crows peck him in flight,
and in our yard, songbirds flee. What is light, shed
from a body of pain? Near the end he was cloaked in bruise,
blue as evening sky. And in his small room—a flickering—
not mystery—maybe a moth—the essential him—morphing
his limbs into wings. So many versions of missing. We
knew for years that death was near, but grief holds us close—
clawed and sharp, small birds clutched in its beak.

Tina Carlson

Headlamp, On

Moon shredding through my tent
at night. I am camped on sand—as in
Leave No Trace. Solid walls

straight up both sides, very dark.
Sudden flood of light from earth's satellite
wakes me every time. Feels like flint.

More like gravity—where we're drawn
together by forces greater than our own when
combined. Where every action has

its equal and opposite reaction. Both repelled
and attracted at the same time by laws
of physics neither can explain. Get up,

pull the boots on, go relieve myself in the river.
Shadows appear next to boulders.
Cliff sides clear as day loom. Animals watch.

Nancy Christopherson

Mather Point

There's something about standing out here
railed in against the abyss, watching the Geminids
at 2 a.m., the Big Dipper flipped over and Orion,
as always, dazzling with physique and shield,

bright Betelgeuse, sword hung, and the blurry
nebular gasses glowing green to my naked eye.
Gemini's Twins lie farther west and Cass is way
down north. Summer's constellations are long gone,

having swung around to the opposite side of Earth.
I think of the deep pitted slabs of limestone on
which I plant my fanny to observe and sometimes
lean back against. So good to have binoculars

along for the favorites—nebulae and star clusters—
dear Andromeda who will chew us a new one
for supper one fine evening distant. Possibilities
for collision are limitless. From here I can see

Phantom quite easily, the occasional swing of
headlamps bound for the toilet or perhaps striking
out early for hitting the trail. One or two lights
at the ranch or the station. Someone's always up

down there, someone sick or injured or needing
attention or just out stargazing and breathing, maybe
looking for scorps, using their black lights. Crazy.
Get some sleep! The constant roar of the river

flowing past. But seated here or lying down flat
looking up, where the whole sky dome is open and the
meteors zip and zing and arc through the dark,
across the deep midnight-blue cloak, heavy with stars

and the longer, higher uplift of the North Rim
stretched horizontally, lucid and ink-black against
the silence, I can lose myself entirely in a place
like this, where humans temporarily out-number

by thousands the critters who fortunately sleep mostly
out of sight. Where the gray fox will startle the
daylights out of me screaming from a tree, where
one big cat will spray scent all over my gear,

into the rock clefts. Exquisite mastery at the sight
of me. Where the cliffs close in but don't close
me in. Where I'm completely vulnerable and truly
alone with the genesis of this precise moment.

Nancy Christopherson

Accident Report

Look out that window—the one facing the sun.
See how the light falls, softly cool and clean
upon the site of last night's hit-and-run
when winter side-swiped spring, then fled the scene.
Let's reconstruct what happened by examining
the scraps of snow left on the budding plums,
and interrogate the bees now browsing
above our icy yellow cactus blossoms.
Fresh snow across eastern mountain slopes
still winks into the clear blue lens of air.
We should put aside our fears and hopes
and go down to that small café, where
we'll order eggs with chile green and red
because it's Christmas in March, the seasons said.

Stan Crawford

Writing on Earth and Sky

Water's signature, carved canyons,
unsigned graffiti: *I was here.*

At dusk just outside Carlsbad,
from a cave, the bats erupt,
a flying stream of flapping black
against the sky, an endless emptying
that flows midair in tandem with a river,
follows every turn, a pouring
out of earth that whirls and clouds
and fills nearly an hour.

Time we measure in days,
the work of eons.

Chill reaches my perch on a wind-worn rock;
I watch, wrapped in my red blanket,
the salt spread across dark sky,
the girth of the Milky Way
that holds me.

Cheney Crow

West Texas, the Big Bend

Driving west, towards the Pecos, the sky widens.
Vegetation shrinks: live oaks disappear in the rearview,
along with the juniper, persimmon, cedars, madrone;
they back down, shading hills, agaritas' young lemony
spring leaves, tart in the mouth, soft to swallow,
not hard yet, not thorned at the tips.

Past the Pecos, where the horizon spreads,
water's erosion yields crust-coated sea creatures,
dinosaur tracks. Bones of all ages, fox-prints, javelina, furred scat
of a mountain lion. Word is, *If you see it, you're not lunch.*

In the Chisos, sudden mountains rise from the desert floor,
junipers reappear, face down the Río Grande,
striated canyons, yellow-green tuff, a pass named for Mule Ears.
Here astronauts learned to read rocks' geological turns.

In a single night, twenty-six galaxies touch me.

Silent, a great horned owl watches.
I lie in thin water. Time
stretches. It does not heal.

History gathers the sky over night-crossings, canyons,
the river road, spiked ocotillo. A crescent moon rises.

Cheney Crow

Sleeping with a Calf

Although the night is dust-blurred
and whisper-filled, her small feet
find the path to the barn
and the crying calf.
All day it called into vacancy.
Pulled too soon from its mother,
it wobbles on knobby legs,
stretches its neck to watch
the girl climb over the sides
of the worn wooden stall.
Its flat nose nudges her side
as she cradles its chunky head
and smoothes curls between
its large black eyes. Together
they fall back into sweet summer
hay and sleep. The girl's arm curves
over its furred side, which rises
and falls with heavy sighs. The calf
pulls her fingers into its toothless
mouth gaining nothing of sustenance,
only a baby's sense of comfort.
Both are innocent sacrifices.
The newly-born calf growing
toward market; the girl losing
her mother to a man's promises.
But tonight in the cold stall
of a cavernous barn, love flares
like a small lantern holding back
their shadowed futures. The blowing
sand scratches the roof's dome,
mourning doves feather the rafters
while cows chew a lullaby of straw.
The nearby horse lowers its huge head,
breathes a breath of warmth over
the sleeping bodies. In the dark,
who could tell calf and girl apart?

Carolyn A. Dahl

Midnight Topography

Tonight I want to explore you in the dark,
     I tell him and search for his arm,
twirl into the curve of elbow,
     roll into the warmth of his chest.
I place both palms,
     twin stethoscopes of sense,
on the rise of muscles,
     probe for the throb of pulse
from a heart I tell him is mine alone.

When he laughs, throws back his trickster
     head, I slip under his chin,
fit into a space undiscovered before.
     With his jawbone on the plateau
of my skull, I ask him to say his name
     slowly, like an enchantment.
I want to feel the moment he begins
     as sound, vibrations rising up
his coyote throat, overpowering
     the flamboyance of tongue,
and catching in the curiosity of my ears,
     those strange sculptures
of the head, bone forgotten.

When the Seven Stars glow in our skylight,
     my foot slides the measure
of his leg, and my toes dip into the hollows
     of his feet, vacancies I believe
were mine to fill. Connected like pinions
     in the dark, my arm traces
the hard architecture of hips
     as I brush his lips, taste the wine
from the bottle I had saved, when I
     thought I knew everything
about him, that he was a geography
     of unchangeable points in
a mapped future no morning light
     could ever rearrange.

Carolyn A. Dahl

When the Gravity of Sorrow Overwhelms

On a restless night, leave your house

and go alone to a garden of always flowers.

Lie down in the grace of the horizontal

and listen to the gritty melodies of tunneling

roots that know nothing of surface affairs.

Confess everything to the growing syllables

of stems. Stare at the white eye of the bone moon.

Believe it loves you best. Believe moonlight

is a lost spell you've been chosen to sing.

When light gathers on your lips like notes,

sing softly to soothe yourself, or loudly to throw

your sorrows over the crowns of sunflowers.

While Earth holds you safely on her curved

hip, roll over to the lizard smell of soil

where another world, oblivious to your weight,

moves below your cheek. Then sleep in the drugged

scent of flowers until the burning sun breaks

into the bedroom of night, and you rise again

humming into the height of your vertical life.

Carolyn A. Dahl

Sunset Blues

My shadow drags along, stretching thin as rope so I press forward, hoisting its length around my weary shoulder, a loose noose I'd sooner use to lasso you, heart, who makes camp in a creek or Saguaro bed simply to discourage me. Think again, love. I've decamped in Buckskin Gulch. Sucked venom from scored rattlesnake bite. Shot that frothing coyote you outran. Campfire legends, you and I, Gruff and Stumble.

Margo Davis

Staycation

The two of us—reliving
our Glen Canyon camping trip

as he thrashes and rolls toward
a rickety fence skirting our alley.

He gasp-snores, our tent tipping
toward an obvious fault line,

another rift. ZZZ. Our money
blown this go-round on scratch cards

and Lay's Sour Cream and Onion.
I prefer Zapp's Voodoo Chips.

Tight-fisted rocks shift beneath me
and within. I recall flirting with

the great abyzzz on a cliff-hanging
white-knuckle road as he had

pointed to the gorgeous sunset.
His snore travels up stiff canvas

like a zzzerrated knife. I fight off
an urge to stifle his breath, roll

him toward the collapsing fence.
Pointy stars spill in, pricking him.

Margo Davis

not yet

Bryce Canyon, Utah, Spring Equinox, 2024

mere shadows, the ancient, striated hoodoos pose
above this snowy valley, while a corporeal vernal chill
strains now for a sudden intrusion

from a planet's gentle turn   *unzip but not in tick-tock
cadence,* I pray: the raven must still repair
her dark and iridescent barbules

the canyon's yawning wrap of jagged
conifers prepare their daily debut but I'll
not gently let the darkness go, when you go—

when cancer spits out crude victory   the night
will not predict your sorrow of parting;
only light can corrupt this comfort

of ambiguity, so please, do not mutter
the dawn—not now/not ever
so softly   what comes is so much more

than sun   I dread the fragile, ragged moment
just before the stars pop off
I am not a morning person;

I put off the garb of a mourning person
I'm coffee now—no sugar/no cream—
vampiric and not the least diurnal

yet subtraction comes so stubbornly fast;
resist the unzipping just a bit longer
mute the rattling song of busy

starlings—this
inevitable reveille for I'm
not ready for that steady glare,

exposing me—exposing
your approaching absence—
absenting the pall   please,

not yet

Terry Dawson

when only a rosary will do

Austin, Texas, Good Friday, 2024

with ghostly nearly unnoticed aplomb,
aping graveside umbrellas folding one by one,
dozens of cormorants cluster at dusk
on the banks of the Lower Colorado

the tangled bald cypresses, whose roots grip tight
the fragile caliche of shrinking soil, gather these
pelagic silhouettes like beads to thumb
a twilight prayer—each bird: a felt *Hail Mary*

red crepuscular dust with the day's weight now
settles in the crevices of everything
all our wings are weary
all our eyes grow dim

our sins, ever before us,
wash thin in the scrubbing darkness
soon we'll dream of wriggling fish
in our scissorbills that gently, gently

press firm to point the way and lift us
high in the bloodied light so unashamed to die—
to free us from tedious study of ourselves as we
get lost in the counting of our feathered strokes,

approaching once more the maw of tomorrow
we, now Icarus in reverse, leave the sun to itself—
find ourselves in the dark, tear temple veils apart
again and again and again

Terry Dawson

Obsidian Petals, Nopales Bloom

Gathering dark unravels our fears in silent swoon beneath bruised skies

Nopales lean like wachadores, spines rattling estrella dust
A niña drifts past gated doorways—braids of obsidian, eyes flickering ember

Traffic fractures puddles—
tired conquistadors crack beneath tires
A stray dog barks its warning; tamales steam in the glow of a lone streetlamp

Gathering dark devours our secret prayers in silent swoon

La sombra antigua coils through callejones at the slam of iron gates
Spines of nopales flex—a chorus in whispered náhuatl

A niña's laughter blooms in the gathering dark
Petals crawling ghosts drift crimson on cracked asphalt
Her voice, un susurro de esperanza, threads through our familia's veins

Gathering dark unravels our doubts in silent bloom

Bajo la luna vieja, nopales stand guard—sentinels draped in moonlight
She reaches out—fingers brushing cactus needles, sparks of futuro

Gathering dark is devoured in afecto's flare
We push back the night with risas y coraje
And a niña's laughter blooms in the gathering dark

Marcial Delgado

The Thunderbird

Sitting on cool concrete, my back against a cinder block wall
I wait for the sun to sink low enough for the projector to roll,
for moving color beyond the swing set, slide, merry-go-round.

I like watching from here. A heavy speaker mounted on a
rolled-down window can't compete. Out here my legs stretch
in front of me, my skin on concrete, distractions hushed.

Patrons enter the glow around the corner behind me,
leaving with cokes in waxy cups, Milk Duds, popcorn. Before
the movie's end, our car lures me from the desert chill.

Suddenly headlights flash white into the night.
Mom waits her turn to descend the hump, eases
into line, turns east onto Highway 90.

From the farthest back corner of the Chevy wagon,
I strain to see elusive jumping lights
pop up, disappear, reappear, split in two,
disappear again, reappear elsewhere—one here, one
there—mostly south, seldom north. Marfa lights.

Later, drifting into sleep in my twin bed opposite my
sleeping sister, the bouncing lights follow Butch and
Sundance across the desert, sometimes part of
the posse, sometimes whirling on the merry-go-round,
and sometimes so close they can touch them.

Mary Margaret Dougherty

Walking Along the Blanco River During Drought

As light lifts the darkness, the slow current
flows clear over half-buried stones.

Beyond my sight, my father sits in a shadowed
room deciding how much he will refuse today

to eat, to swallow—afraid as he is of filling up,
spilling over. I kneel, reach into the shallows,

guided by hint of color glinting through the muck.
Does surprise take refuge within a riverbed?

Something smooth and solid meets my fingers.
I pull it forth into light, cleansing as I lift:

a red, speckled stone to companion a hand,
give weight to a pocket, stir a faded memory.

The hollow left by my digging holds its edges
until the river, slowed by drought, evens out

all the freshly disturbed places.

Cyra Sweet Dumitru

Dementia: Evaporation

Each day, more of me evaporates.
~ Mother

The last clear splash of
water in the well

soon will evaporate
into today's light.

I will be bone dry.
Utterly empty.

Words already ash
upon my parched tongue.

Let the rain keep its
distance. My arid

cup no longer can
hold. The well fills with

shadows, more felt than
seen. Silence rises

from boundless depths,
washes me with plenty.

When words vanish,
know that I am diving

into shining dust.

Cyra Sweet Dumitru

Dusk, Late October

If you remain in the garden past dusk, snow will cover your body, a statue, white marble, soft. Birds will land on your head. Nests will overcome you. A sparrow with a chestnut underbelly will fold her wings upon your reluctant breath. Her discarded feathers will attach to your shoulder blades while everyone you've ever loved will remember the ways you were kind, the ways you were not. You in the garden, steps from an open door, yellow aspen leaves at your feet. Maybe you will weep. More likely, you will feel the universe in your heart, hear the far-off trembling of a creek in the forest where you once spread your body across warm leaves, felt the sun on your face, remembered the night as a wound &, you, howling to a dark sky.

To forgive is to surrender &,

at the moment of release,

    your new wings will carry you

        into the map of yourself.

Put your finger down,

    anywhere &

      go there,

        go there.

Alicia Elkort

Morning Toast

How can I work today? The sun's out, the lawn
not mown (overgrown!)—but those sunflowers stalk me,

nod blonde heads at the striped cat swishing
their knees, stealthing for field mice. In cottonwoods

crows holler themselves hoarse:
Call! Call! Call!

I know you thought it was *Caw! Caw! Caw!*
You were wrong.

Caw and *Call* sound the same but are different things:
Crows *caw* and you go about your busy-ness. They *call*

and a poem lifts up. Flies. Or tries. Don't judge. It's all song,
after all, some lilt sweeter than others to *your* learned ear.

So, no. Now's no time to toil and spin. This poet
has something to crow about—given those sparrows,

that field, these sunflowers, this day—
Yes, this day.

Kelly Ann Ellis

When light gathers on your lips like notes,
sing softly to soothe yourself, or loudly to throw
your sorrows over the crowns of sunflowers.

Carolyn A. Dahl

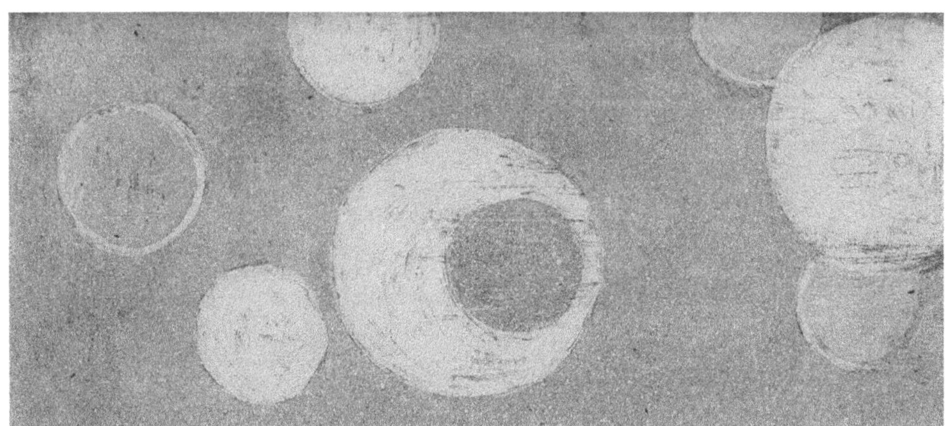

A Fossilized Footing

Dusk settles in
As nighthawk wing beats
Push the darktide
Closer to ground

The air is loud
With monsoon fragrance as
Wet sandstone releases
Time-compressed spices

Sage and juniper
Ride on tangerine rays
My eyes aren't sure
If they see or smell it

Pneet, Pneet

The nighthawk patrols
Swooping and scooping
Mouthfuls of high desert bugs
Even Time stops for the show

My brother Tom and I
Watch from the patio
Grounded on sandstone slabs
We hauled from the quarry

The dusty stone worker's
Eyes had given us
A long look
Then danced a bit

He pushed a chunk our way
We puzzled at patterns
Indentations trailing
Across the solid sand

Tom's eyebrows arched,
Fossilized footprints?
A smile parted the dust
On the man's face

A special offering
From an old soul
Tom laid the slabs
Showcasing the tracks

He a wise twenty-five
Me, twenty years old
Going on twelve
All my ligaments loose

But that nightfall
I found a footing
Resting with Tom
In sandstone footprints

Nancy Fine

The sound of wings not beating

In gray light
soft as the paws
of a cat,
the mourning
dove won't find
her tongue.
How I long
for the comfort of
the stuffed mother
they gave the rescued
nestlings to calm them.
If we could sleep
with the sound of a heart
not beating,
would we finally learn
to fly? This morning
the snow fell muted
on the mountains till
I could not tell the trees
from the silence
between them.

Stacey R. Forbes

Zest

In this kitchen, I zest winter lemons for you. The zester slips.
I am happy to bleed because I am happy to breathe.

The coyote sings with terrible tenderness to streetlamps
and fathers whose names are the very same as silence.

For now, the fires are too far away to see by—so we sit
together in the dark. We laugh to push back against gravity,

love to cauterize the flaming trees. Our bodies purple
with the wordless fall of Mexican piñons, mothers, and stars.

The table holds up the plate. The knife. The rind curled in loss.
We still have the sea. There is infinite salt for these wounds.

Stacey R. Forbes

In the end, cosmology comes down to the study of flowers

How does it feel
to be so small?
This multiverse of wailing
stars a quilt
not vast enough
to hold any two of us
together.

What does it mean
to be without measure?
A cluster of buds
on a century
plant, quiet and still
unopened, holding up
the moon.

Stacey R. Forbes

Overheated

How long does it take coffee to sit until it becomes stale?
How long does it take to sit until we run out of things to say?
Does one stay sitting until darkness comes—
pretend to be statues, stone-blood, fooling the mosquitos?

I am willing to sit here until I forget the last words we said.
I am willing to repeat them again—but the road is warm
even if we're cold, and you need to leave—
go to where mountains melt into desert,

and the radio doesn't even have voices
but the static in between stations
like the words we meant to say
but stalled too long, and the engine turned cold.

Heather D Frankland

Song of Respite

The plaintive cry of the chachalaca at dusk,
the echolocations of bats in the invisible air,
starving for wild fruits swallowed in black.
Your necklace tinkling like a tiny church,
like Saint Jude's, that little adobe mission
slumped darkly on a hill by the Río Grande.
We had spied it as we rose out of the water, dripping,
orange blossom breezes drying our legs.

Your face bears sorrow like an ancient cross.
We don't pray for miracles, only a chance.
It would be nice, making a living, doing Easter
in your family's village in San Luis Potosí,
returning for graduation cookouts in the park.

Men in masks haunt the stores, schools, even
the shrine of Nuestra Señora de San Juan del Valle.
We sneak inside, entering through the sanctuary.
The votive candles don't light, and I'm a mess.
You smile, striking a match with your teeth.

The waning moon is a ghostly grimace shrinking.
We run like young lovers under the cover of night.
We hold hands, and it's enough to know
that you are here, too, now, and breathing.

Belén Thérèse Garza Flores

From the Book of Revelation: Knowledge

I learned why the sky was blue
and why the rain smelled so sweet,
like fresh yellow corn, like the Mazatzal
Mountains in spring, as we drove nonstop,
sleeping at rest areas in the car.

I learned to drive standard, to dance huapango,
pick sweet watermelon, speak Spanish,
avoid paying collect calls, avoid tolls,
read paper maps like young adult novels.

And I gasped, rising one pink morning,
seeing the red sun rise like a heart between peaks,
seeing that night was done—now was the time for light,
excessive warmth, and greeting a lover.

And you arose, anxious to make good time,
and the ribbons in my hair waved with devotion,
and my limbs ached with time and want.

Belén Thérèse Garza Flores

Song of Thomas Walks Easy

When the cold nose of Sammy
my rescue Chihuahua, nuzzles
my neck I begin to rouse, lift my blanket
for him to wriggle under,
when he is wakeful-warm and pokes
his ice-cube nose in my back,
I hear your song smooth as a lover's whisper,
know to turn on the light,
to get up, to find slippers,
check the weather this frigid
Albuquerque winter morning,
when I am out of bed, out of my warm,
ready to face the dark and biting cold,
we descend the stairs

when I'm covered so the neighbors
won't accidentally see me
in my night clothes,
when he is sweatered and leashed,
we venture into the freezing dark and quiet,
so he may make his first offering
to the grass gods,
when we come back inside, he
runs up the stairs, curls
in the still warm blankets
sleeps until after sunrise,

when I make my coffee,
sit at the table, watch the dark
fade to light, absorb the desert
dawn as I write of the dog,
my day yet to be, I hear your song
of crows, of life, of what is yet to come
when the quiet will steal you away.

Lenora Rain-Lee Good

Desert Stalker

Gila monster rests
in the stolen burrow
once home to rabbit and kits—
now bone and blood and beads
of the Gila monster. Now
part claw and fang
of the desert—
no longer blind, helpless prey.

Sands still warm from
sun of day, night cool air
calls Gila to stir, waddle toward
scent of next prey trail,
tongue flickers, searches
for mouse or lizard, quail, egg,
or tortoise, anything he can ambush
or corner.

Strong jaws lock over flesh
and bone, venomous
saliva grinds into meat
and blood—liquid lava, pure
paralyzing pain,
incapacitating pain. David's
soldiers over Uriah.

There is no escape.

Lenora Rain-Lee Good

7 a.m.

A small fox greets me beyond the porch
as I stand stretching, arms raised
to the setting moon, a bright eucharist
beaming through the trees,
sliding down the morning.
One little kit following, then another,
a new litter this season.

Like hobos riding the rails,
who mark the fence of a house
with a cat drawing to signal
kind lady lives here—she'll feed you,
these kits have heard about me.

I go out to fill the birdbath,
then the feeders,
in a prodigal spilling of sunflower seeds
on the ground, where they can find it,
where their mother has told them
to look.

Martha K. Grant

Restless

Drawn to the back porch by night sounds
that blanket the dark, I've stumbled
into a meditation-in-progress.
In the temple of oaks and cedars,
a congregation of treefrogs
is chanting a call-and-response.

Like the uninitiated in the balcony,
witness to a form of worship
in a culture not my own,
I stand in awe, timing
the cadence of my breath
to the trill of their
unfamiliar prayer, adding
my own quiet *Om*
into the night.

Martha K. Grant

Mystery, or the Certainty of Wonder

The third time he gets up
to pee, it's almost dawn,
best chance to look out the windows
to see deer chew alfalfa
(despite his best efforts
it grows as a weed in the red soil),
or foxes dig in the compost,
or rats gathering seed under the bird feeders,
and bored raccoons
apparently just looking for something to do.

Morning starts as a gray wet gel
over Cat Mesa; piñon, dark silhouettes,
lift the day.
He restarts the fire in the stove
with paper and pitch and sticks of juniper
under a piece of ponderosa.
Thick smoke hangs over his yard
before the fire takes,
or wind blows it away.

Even parallel lines touch,
at infinity; distance collapses—
also known as a vanishing point,
he remembers.

Benjamin Green

Like Fire

He thought he would go outside
To watch the moon,
But it was too cold:
Stars glittered like ice
Over the mesa tops.

And, then to the east,
After he went back inside:

The moon rose,
Isolated in the sky,

A slivered arch over ponderosas—
The glow
Burning the sky
Like fire.

He watches a raven
Descend to darkness,
Gliding on opened wings.

Benjamin Green

Auditorium

On the banks of the Blanco
in a turquoise casita
I wake to the opening notes
of a symphony—

    chickadees
    painted buntings
    black-crested titmice
    brown-headed cowbirds
    golden-cheeked warblers
    mockingbirds who echo them all.

Music fills this venue of live oak and cedar,
reaches its ceiling of dawn-soft blue.

I've come to this place to recover from cancer
and discovered a concert hall.

Amy L. Greenspan

Mourning Dove

Pink light, scented by sage
slips through shutters

stripes the bedroom
liquifies—

you are gone

I am a balsa vessel
drifting hollow

past bald cypress
mesquite-thorned hills

Float or sink?

The mourning dove's waking call
tells me I must rise

lift from her primrose crib
the child

who wears your eyes.

Amy L. Greenspan

What Passes for Silence in Alamogordo

Nothing in the room is innocent.
Not the chair, not the sock,
not the slow-spreading light
that touches everything without asking.

A bird hesitates outside,
unsure whether to sing.
The air smells like reheated bathwater,
and something half-alive in the walls.

Across the lot, a truck door slams.
Boots drag across gravel.
An engine turns, then stalls.
AM gospel leaking through the static.

Someone once buried something here
that never stopped humming.
Paint peels toward it.
Even the sink leans a little west.

Clothes are gathered from the chair.
A sock with a hole.
Nothing waits.
Still, the boots go on.

The light reaches the table,
finds the corner of a map
and a name written in someone's else's hand.

Ben Griffin

Armadillo Adagio

Darkness casts an open hand.
So begins the overture as
bats divide the dusky sky, then
fireflies rise like wraiths

against curtains of night,
notes of light and dark.
Catch the crickets crooning,
in their sopranos.

Treefrogs the size of thimbles
carol an alto line, threading
we are here, we are here.
Again, again.

A sharp retort of buckfight,
the flop-splash of fish,
turkeys squabble-gobble,
sort themselves to roost.

The chitter of kingfisher
patrols the river. Owl call
and response. Call and response.
Armadillo bulldozes dry leaves.

Porcupines trill their whereabouts.
Nocturnal means loud.
Darkness mends.
Let us fold our wings and listen.

Lucy Griffith

God as Darker Dark in a Night Blizzard

I have never seen him kneel.

Zero degrees minus wind chill.
I carry my offering in his pan—
maple sugar frosted shredded wheat.
Blowing snow. The car idles, shines headlights on the gate.
Squeeze myself through.
What do farmers do?
What do I know?
Love for this horse unstitches me.

I seek a darker dark in the night snow.
No, it's a bush.
Now I am leaping, floating a bit, trying to hold steady
the treat. Another bush. Snowfield rolling like a wave.

He will be a darker dark in the blizzard.

I dreamed his mother came to me,
a white spirit horse, grulla,
and she said, *Take care of my son.*
In the dream, I told David about it
and as I spoke, I cried.
I thought I had been called
for the mustang people.

I loved one horse.
I lay my hands on his scars;
I heard him nicker when I was not there.
He showed me time and earth
move like music when we stood still.

Carol D Guerrero-Murphy

Waking Near Winter Solstice

My friend wore a red dress as we hiked across
a dry grass field, sere brown, the dress a poppy, a flag,
a bird. As I woke, I thought we had been marching
and now it's dawn a few mornings shy of winter's solstice.
More gray than light. Frost lightens from black to white
as I watch, then finally, a goldening, a pinking, wing
of a rosy finch. What is heavy moves off, retreats east
as even in the cold there is a quickening, waves
of love for the beginning of colors, a reason to untangle
from my blankets, place my feet on the floor and stand.
My heart determines to beat, my lungs to fill.
Another bit of color shines off a glass window.
A life raft of color floating on the night sea, a destination
I can swim to, brighter and brighter, rose and gold.

Carol D Guerrero-Murphy

First Notes

Like an orchestra tuning
for the grand concerto,
early morning sounds
in a desert city
play in sections.

First, peacocks squawk,
then sirens screech,
doves mourn,
a garbage truck bangs.

Before the sun blares full
over the Sandias,
the neighbor's two dachshunds
bark shrill alarms.

With piccolo notes
of a truck in reverse,
it's time to open my eyes,
roll over and whisper
love tones to the silent
mound beside me.

Sheryl Guterl

Rachmaninoff under the Stars

Hear swelling strings, accented
with riveting piano keys,
and the timpani too.

I sit stone-still—
my head tilted back, eyes
transfixed on nothing

when a large, dark bird,
an owl I guess,
floats silent, surreal

through my sight—
and I am reminded that darkness
has its own vision

of things unforeseeable.
I listen and I feel
and I believe

in the truth of everything,
even lies
which have a truth of their own.

Ken Hada

Evening, Arizona

Desert plants bloom wildly
while the calendar still says Winter.
The sun is already pre-heating the valley
before the overwhelming summer blast.

Sunset calls the wild things
from their long afternoon siestas;
evening summons baskets
of bright stars in an infinite sky.

The quail have gone to roost,
safe from coyotes on the hunt.
A pale full moon rises as I walk the dog
one last time before dark.

Distracted by the silence, I forget,
for the moment, the ongoing surprises
of arriving in this unexpected place
and learning to call it home.

C. T. Holte

Footnote

Asterisk is a fancy way to mark a star on paper. The night's a brimming cup of thirst, big and little dippers poised against an ebony felt that glitters like dew. They say you can't go home again? But here you are. Before an *I* or even an inkling, you were part star, jettisoned matter coalescing as well to karst and kale, landscapes of grief and joy. Part lucky meteor, smeared with amino acid and splashing down into your nursery.

Your origin is a mystery unsolvable through photons and pupils. Think instead of charm and strange, quark and anti-quark. Color charges. It's not enough that you rotate the whole solar system as if it's tethered to you. Think beyond the Cartesian: why not a universe? Past Uranus' distant rings and the volcanic eruptions of Io to whole galaxies' black holes shooting X-rays as they gobble their neighbors. By the time you remember what you meant to say, the full moon's at zenith as a meteorite arcs over the lip of the mesa.

Cindy Huyser

Superbloom

After the downpour,
before first light slips
the scant horizon, dormant seeds
begin to wake, embryos patient
as desert toads who'd waited
out a decade's drought
to throat desire loud
as hallelujahs at a tent revival.

The torrent scrubbed
the canyon with its own loose
-rooted trees, sweeping
rabbits, deer, human beings
unaware of its imminent power.

My room glows, goes dark
with news of Earth's indifference,
cruelty coming into flower.
Some tadpoles hatched today
will devour others. The landscape
takes on rose tones, subtle
shifts in color. What earth
inside me will I tend,
what seeds water?

Cindy Huyser

The Nothing That Is

> *. . . nothing himself, beholds*
> *Nothing that is not there and the nothing that is.*

> ~ Wallace Stevens, "The Snow Man"

Remove yourself from society—
set up permanent camp
in the desert, the mal país
of New Mexico, say—
and behold the loss of self,
identity theft and you the thief.

Senses persist: you see
the black stones, so sharp,
you think you can
taste them, and the scent
of piñon and stunted cedar
strong enough to lift
you into these mountains.

Now you can feel
the mass of desert night
descend upon your encampment:
it is both light—enormous stars—
and heavy, the weight
of moon struggling, aching to rise.

D. Iasevoli

Too Far Gone

Let's stay awake all night, to guarantee
we don't sleep through our flights, I say,
and so we talk and love and eat,
catalogue our stops the past three days—
those towns whose names evoke
our own exhausted, enchanted minds—
Alamogordo, Quemado, Carrizozo.
I drift; I fall asleep. Near dawn, you invite
me outside to falling snow, soft alchemy,
as it sighs above Ten Thousand Waves,
our nest, and we gaze in silent joy.
I want to drop to my knees, and pray
to you, but we drive to Albuquerque
for our separate flights, to separate deserts.

D. Iasevoli

Hospice (Aspen)

Genetically identical trees sprout as a single organism out of one of earth's oldest living beings. The aspen clone can remain alive, dormant, until it detects an ideal balance of sun and moisture and nutrients in air and soil. This hospice is for Pando, the largest and oldest of the clones, dying in Utah.

In all this time we were here, drought resisters,
I've waited too for a savior, a poem
To love the trees with, all the sunrise of our minds
Breaking as waking into pure announcement.
No hard feelings, you told me. When I came back
I thought if I made myself small that might work,
If I could let myself be apprehended
As the mud in my heart, tarantula egg,
A brutal blue. Clarity invites the dull
Hill to appear shining, wrapped with bandages.
Your bluebird, red-naped sapsucker, tree swallow.

Joy Jacobson

Rest Home, Jemez Springs

Down where
The stream widens, the whole world
Alluvial, and water spreads to fingers like a hand,
There's a glint in glass and a woman
Behind it holding forth
The daily ceremony, bread to bird. She cranks,
Widdershins, the window open. Dawn
Air rushes her and her blue mug,
Adobe wall, Saltillo floor, her parents' lined
Faces framed in refashioned oak.
Sand shimmers at the bottom of a blue glass pot.
Eggs boil against it; as clouds hang
Rain above the cliff, river moves
Ice toward summer. She endures
The bird-flight of her sentences sheared
Cold by these forces
And slices the orange flesh of a squash, arranging it
On a rust-red plate
As though all her life had been stilled, a triptych, oil
On pine: knife, body, opening.

Joy Jacobson

Hourglass

The Carolina wren returned
last night. She slept beneath
the front porch eave, leaving
before the sun could find its way
to my door.

The honeybees have left their hive.
They wait in line for the hibiscus
to open her blooms. I wake
to hummingbird wings or the hum
of my neighbor's mower,

sounds made by the door of sleep
opening to morning. I glimpse
your silhouette framed in my bedroom
window, your hourglass figure,
a memory of time running out.

Mark Jodon

On the Way to Santa Fe

In the morning when I look at him
lying in bed, not awake yet, he looks
no different than before, but I know now
why he keeps forgetting we're going to Santa Fe.

We will rise and drink coffee, pack up the car,
check out of the Safari Motel in Tucumcari,
skip the interstate, take the less-traveled road
through the canyonlands up to Las Vegas.

The morning light magnifies everything,
making clear the long path ahead, the switchbacks
up mountains, the scenic turnouts at the top where
we can look back and see where we have traveled.

We wind through a canyon where a herd of horses
gallops free across the landscape. I long to be
with them, running free, running away from darkness,
running into the crystalline light.

At Las Vegas we take the interstate toward Santa Fe
and he turns to me, smiling. *I'll always remember
how pretty those horses looked running,* he says.
In that light, I add. The light that clarifies everything.

Kathryn Jones

Nightfall on the Edge of the West

The notched horizon glows like an ember
against the evening redness

while I stand on the limestone ledge
looking west, wondering who lives

in the house with a yellow porchlight,
the only human sign I'm not alone.

The crescent moon hangs on an ebony branch,
clouds caught on the thorns while

a white-tailed buck crowned in velvet
emerges from the woods to nibble corn

I have thrown on the ground as I do
every evening, knowing he will come.

White-winged doves take off with
a distinctive wing whistle,

a rattlesnake stretches across the gravel road,
absorbing the last heat of the day.

The yellow porchlight blinks off,
the buck wanders back into the woods,

the doves fly over the horizon,
the rustling, slithering, stalking begins.

Howls and hoots and growls rise
from the darkness, calls of the wild

telling me the night is not empty, but alive
and I am part of it, never alone, never lonely.

Kathryn Jones

Winter Solstice at Sunset

Amber light outlines the Sangre de Cristo Range,
a solemn oath to dark. Clouds tuck in their nimbus
and block the stars. I sit inside, inhale blue ink,
wish for a tomorrow clear enough to hike
the West Peak, its purple breath, green sleeves,
white snowcap.

There's a bit of mountain in all of us, but tonight
I'm full of barbed wire, séance, and prickly cactus,
chatting with the dead. Though they never speak,
they can chill a room with their once-upon-a-time breath.
They can waft in and out pages of window curtains
like invisible ink.

Even clouds, clothed in burnish and glaze, still ramble
after midnight—their scatter and shed, their horsetails
and cirrostratus halos. Some wear veils, others billow,
but for now darkness has kidnapped them, won't release
them until sunrise. I'll wait for dawn, the first shadow
and name it *Umbra*.

Kate Kingston

Sunrise Pantoum

Something has to be said for the red
stitches that hold the pages together
in the center crease of my notebook.
Shifts in light change everything.

Stitches hold the pages together
as dawn weaves dark to day.
Shifts in light change everything,
loosen gravity from its pull.

As dawn weaves dark to day.
I wake in my mother's cornfield,
loosen gravity from its pull,
yellow-green tassels higher than my head.

I wake in my mother's cornfield,
a maze of shadows, a place to get lost,
yellow-green tassels higher than my head.
No skyline, no road, no internet, no cell.

A maze of shadows, a place to get lost,
to break trails through stalks and leaves.
No skyline, no road, no internet, no cell,
just me and acres of ears listen

to trails break through stalks and leaves,
traverse roots, slip between elbows.
Just me and acres of ears listen
to harvest. The wind's insistent rustle

traverses roots, slips between elbows.
Something has to be said for the red
harvest, wind's insistent rustle
in the center seam of my notebook.

Kate Kingston

Willows on St. Brigid's Day

Sun pinks the sandy wash,
threads a narrow path
through steep bank's shadow,

among gray branches
traces palest green
on earth-brown buds.

> First of February,
> feast day of St. Brigid, midwife,
> protector of hearths and springs
>
> born on the threshold, they say,
> half in the room
> half in the wide wild.

Fluff like down, hulls the faintest flush
like a shell
a rabbit's ear, an infant's mouth,

like itself,
hard brown casing
half off, still clinging,

fingers over softness—
these buds,
this willow fresh in dry places—

my face, too, a sweep of blush,
a fresh anointing
on winter-bitten skin.

Sarah Kotchian

Beaver Moon

During beaver moon
I don't sleep well, dream-tossed,
winter coming, world turning.

Beavers know to build
a dam on water,
come up for air inside.

Golden aspens
hold the last of evening.
In moonlight,

leaves shaped like hearts
fall in full flame,
rain down

on sky-strewn earth.
I am learning
where to find the air.

Sarah Kotchian

Lullaby at Bat Colony Bridge, Tucson, Arizona

Forget the stories of rabies.
The adults   fly from this place
race   the blue hour   winged shapes
periwinkled sky   trace the Rillito
a charcoal river   metallic stars

but here at my feet
there is this   left behind
baby bat   fallen   from beam
the lost grip   the tiny claws.

Imagine   a fairy changeling   ankle-height
shape-shifted   into skin and fur
twin obsidian gleams   two black beads   staring back.

Forget the books   about vampires
even if   there is something
wolverine   in the small face.

I   who never wanted   children
long   to cradle   this fallen imp
infant wings   opening   webbed span
unfolds   wraps itself
     around   my index finger.

Forget the wolfberry and devil's claw.
The parents have flown
hunting   mosquitoes
the night sky   sings   high-pitched
sonar   insects   echolocation
and here in my hand   the tremble   of tiny wings.

Gabrielle Langley

Tracking the Río Grande

This morning a white heron
    its thin neck gently arching
        to and fro, wades along the shore
of the Río Grande, a silhouette in clear sun,

my inclination
    is to know the exact heron, its due
        coloration, habitat, and food,
but soon its awkward grace

suffices. For an hour
    or more I follow the opposite path
        along the river, duck beneath
cottonwoods, brown leaves clacking

in the breeze, keep an eye
    on the heron's calm progress. Sticker
        grass clings, tall water weeds
ripple. I stop each time she stops, an odd

stick protruding from the muddy bank,
    and when she steps again through
        the ooze it comes, it seems, between
my toes. On we go at our slow pace

in the luminous air. Bound by our mutual
    watching: I her, she her prey across the current.
        When, finally, she rises and tries her wings
we both are sun-drenched and shimmering.

   Gayle Lauradunn

Going Not Gently

As the sun sets, the musicians
begin tuning their instruments:
wings scrape against serrated wings,
abdomens shake and rattle.
Then it begins—the tune inscribed
in DNA millennia ago, played fresh
each summer evening,
a simple song: *I
am here.
I am here, come
find me, I am
here, come find me.
Night falls, and still I
am here. Come,
find me.
I am here.*

Eileen Lawrence

When The Sun Returns

After the night-long circuit
that redeems the death-dark
turned and turning face of earth,
at last, the sun approaches the rim
of my heart's awareness
sending before, like heralds,
the graceful, grace-filled
radiance, the pre-dawn
glow of coming change, sky
sliding from darkest blue
to a still uncertain gray, to pearl,
then flaring into jets of crimson,
purpled where clouds stream
and float, a blur of freshest green,
new life leafing, where earth
and light conjoin,
pale rose, silvered wine
on the western mountains, then
transparent gold, washing out
all else, shades to a yellow
unwatchable blaze,
and the molten sun flares
in the east at the threshold
of my soul's dawn until I can look
no longer.

Suzanne Lee

Night Medicine

Rising before dawn with sleep
a distant image unattained,
I cross the shadowed hall
to seek the watching window,
companion of sleepless nights,
expect a hazed and starless sky
eclipsed by scudding ash
from forests blazing
two states away upwind,
and find a visitor moon
ascendant, victorious
over smoke and night
and pain, an awkward wedge
of dusty peach riding
the mountain-rimmed
and milky sky.

Suzanne Lee

That Place by the Sea

I'm back in Santa Fe, my love, sitting up in bed
with my coffee cup, the picture of you smiling benignly
from its wooden frame on the nightstand. I always wake
before the sun on this longest day, as I did those many
solstices ago in the rain-soaked Northwest.
You were still asleep that morning, dreaming perhaps
of what was to come, though you could not know what
awaited you, what awaited us. I roused you with a kiss,
told you to dress and led you by the hand down the beach
to the driftwood temple I'd assembled the day before.
As the sun peeked over the Cascades and beamed its rays
like a nimbus over your head, I knelt in the sand, held out
a golden ring and asked, *Alice, will you marry me?*
You said *Yes*, and the sky blazed bright as our dreams.
I'm still here in our big bed, my love, though you are not.
My cup is dry as this high desert since you've been gone.
I make up that you live on as light, as part of the sun
that bakes this drought-starved land. Some days I lie
face-up on the grass to see if I can feel your touch,
and from time to time I dream that you wake me
with a kiss and lead me through the dawn to that place
by the sea where all I can say, all we can say, is *Yes*.

Wayne Lee

Waking in a Dream

I wake before I am killed.
People die in dreams.
People die in real life.
I am myself, and someone else,
someone who does not live in Santa Fe, in the Southwest,
someone younger, thinner, taller,
about to be garroted in a cartel-style execution.
We are standing in a bordello hallway with a low ceiling,
the assassins and I.
I am wearing gray slacks and a blue shirt.
My armpits are wet,
mouth hangs halfway open.
Then I wake up, in the dream.
Waking saves lives.
Am I safe?
Is anyone safe?
Someone, some puta, snaps our picture,
then the image is erased.
Someone threatens to strangle me,
others point guns.
Someone says through crooked teeth *You are going to die*
and I know he is right.
Then I wake up, in real life.
I have been saved by an angel, the little girl skipping down
the hallway through my dream, perhaps.
I am alive—for now.
But I don't know what I've done or who I am.
All I know is I am in my bed, safe in Santa Fe, in the Southwest.
We contain multitudes,
the living and the dead.
We've all been dead before.
We're all just struggling to stay alive,
to be everyone and everything in our dreams.
I am the younger, thinner man with a forest of hair.

I am the mafioso with pantyhose masking my face,
the puta looking on.
I am the concealed handgun, the wire garrotte, the dimly lit room,
the cheap hotel, the sour smell of fear.
I am the little girl in the party dress who shows me to the stairway,
to the exit I seek.
We contain multitudes, the living and the dead.
Perhaps I am dead, an angel.
Perhaps I am the man who pushes too hard,
dreams too much, tries to do the impossible.
Perhaps the hotel is the resting place of my ambition,
the little girl is my lover, trying to lead me away,
to save my life, to escape into the sheltering sky.
Perhaps Santa Fe is the dream, the Southwest, this whole world,
a dream.
People live and die in dreams.
But I am awake now, until I close my eyes again.

Wayne Lee

Another Late Morning in the Life

You are so deep into America you cannot get out.

~ Miriam Sagan

This daily tapestry of images is just scripture, this cup of black coffee a sensuous act, this dusting of snow a reprieve but a stranger nonetheless. The latest news is gospel, tousled, and howls at the moon. The rising sun lords over the dissonance until this room feels like the last outpost of words. Growing older, it's too bad wonder won't shapeshift like it used to—for instance, I wonder if these Sandhill cranes lifting off the bosque keep jazz hours. I wonder how far birds fly across trackless distances to avoid the particulate polluted skies; they resemble excelsior in the high desert winds, their flocks known to burst into quiet salvos of morning peace. I'd give most anything to learn just one secret between the last wild horses of northern Colorado and a starry night or a gust-exhausted hawk and the prey that just eluded him. But here I am back on earth again, Tribes Coffeehouse, reading Miriam's manuscript

late February
decaf Americano
new year of the snake

John Macker

After Neruda

This particular night hit the ground running.
There were star fields of questions, no echo answered,
just this solitude   this exercise in virtues of consciousness.
For you, Neruda, it was the white hot killers of angry Spain
and the Chilean blood of deserts. For me, maybe it is this
old stone house made of legends, the Río Grande running
broad and full, a jungle of a bosque, the lowbrow humor of coyote—
in the whisper of a shooting star parched
from a million light-year crawl across the universe.
Or do the answers come from *the rain that often struck
your words / filling them with holes and birds?*
Some nights I am at a loss for the words
when I should be soused with them or at least
tracking them through the night, across the moon
or up desert rivers to their source.

John Macker

Humorless Lawman

Last night a great horned owl
declared its ulterior presence for
a couple of hours hooting through
our loneliness, a large white shadow
on a bare tree branch high above
us a few nights before solstice. Bringer
of winter. I projected onto him the
gravity of our situation as if owl alone
kept the medicine.   All the voles
and whiptails that would debouch onto the
midnight ground now scampered for cover.
Owl's eyes froze on our addled dogs. Aloof to our
alarms and excursions, it's not as if he
sought succor in the simple wisdom of the tree
      or the hunger of the moon.

My breathing fused me to his air and for a
brief time, it was his world and to inhabit it
was to breathe freely.   Unlike me, he rues nothing
enhances everything. The Hopi consider owl
the humorless lawman, keeping an eye on the Koshare
clowns. Even the dark is slightly phobic and loses
track of death in his presence, shadows warp.
Could there be real peace without owls or cranes
or swallows winging across the sky?
I projected onto him the gravity of this winter
as something more than a paltry seasonal thing and
nothing but the breeze rustled the tree and the
night was as silent as it was efficient except
for his rhythmic hoots, and the dogs carefully
threading through the leaves aware
      they were being watched.

John Macker

Terra Bakes

Evening rises
In the dead hot center of summer
Like a round of damp bread dough
Already punched down twice,
Almost ready for Terra's oven.
The moon a silvery white crescent
Hanging high in the night sky—
Luna surveys her domain,
The ticking sound of earth
—sand, volcanic rock—
As it cools slightly in the semidark.
Never cooling enough
In the roasting high desert heat,
The enchanted land of the Southwest,
Of cactus and ponderosa and chile.
The land of an empty, grand riverbed,
The water gone missing once again.
Luna weeps not for us humans,
Arid as she is in her own frozen orbit,
An eternal day-night spin.
She keeps a cold distance,
Mourning the earth as it turns,
Watching helpless as Terra burns.

Bram MacLihr

Jimson Weed

The old woman in black
tall, thin, leans on her cane
shaped from willow branch
musing on her garden

the spare gravel walk
sandstone rocks whose
shapes she likes
placed as in Zen painting
the weathered gray wood
of door set into
soft fawn earthen roundness
of adobe wall

above to the east
a silver waxing moon appears
over red wrinkled cliffs
of Ghost Ranch

against the garden wall
the great plant clings
spreading broad gray-green leaves
in the cooling dusk
alabaster blooms open
big as a man's hand
under her patient gaze

Jimson Weed she calls it
she has made many paintings
of Jimson Weed, Nightshade
the blossoms deep and drooping
pale Mars-violet or glass-green
in their center

the Yaqui Indian shaman
told her it was poisonous
to whites—dangerous
so she dug them out
yet let a few persist

she scents their delicate fragrance
closing her eyes
her eyesight fading, narrowing with age
feeling the coolness, sweetness of the evening
smiling faintly
she remembers other nights
other flowerings

Gordon Langdon Magill

Where a Settler Settles

They say a true settler never settles down
and that's kind of unsettling. Namely, a human
ragweed variant stalks the southwest . . . common,
airborne, hard to kill, and the following is what I've heard:
his bloodline is thick and inescapable, filled with
unsettling shapes. He protects no one from everyone
but himself and runs unable to function in peacetime.
His fists dissolve lingo. His dirt-clod, hardpacked, walked-on
lockjaw, clasped old-man hands swing a double-sided
sword through the chopfallen morning camps and his birthright
darkens each navigable dawn when he unzips his tent.
He salts a finely ground path of powdered ashes around
his chair to send a warning before a serpent can strike his heel.
He negotiates peace treaties only through a series of mirrors.
He packs his pet wars like dry rations, passes them around
like sticks of gum at whatever bartop keeps him huddled
and warm and whiteknuckling his ancestral change dish.

Jonathan Mahaffie

Superstition

Pima fear this mountain, farmers named it
Superstition—dust from the lower worlds
bound for Phoenix screeching up through its shafts.
Our science club came to practice the craft
of survival—sent in pairs, just two girls
bent in the desert, keeping the fire lit.

When we found a motorcycle headfirst
in a foul pond edged by palo verdes,
helmet bobbing in scum, and a cactus,
twelve-arms, ringed by gnawed horse bones—Oasis
branded in the collapsed stable murky
in the dusk—we knew we were lost. We cursed

the Lost Dutchman, whose ghost surely gave chase
with his *veni-vidi-vici* scrawled map
and bulleted skull down the eroded scarp.
By flashlight we found flat ground, strung our tarp
from a tree, staked the edge tight as a trap.
We told each other as our pulses raced

that someone would find us when the day breaks
since we hunkered cross-fingered in the brush
near those broad peaks vaulted by Orion,
Superstition shaping our horizon.
But first we endured the night's circling hush
sniffing us out before dawn—limp-and-shake

of a flea-bitten coyote who prowled
packless and nipped for scraps with toothless maw.
We didn't know how to face the canine dark—
the nothing-will-save-us but our own hearts—
at fourteen. But we dared to rise drop-jawed
before first light to unleash our feral howls.

Dawn Manning

The Saguaro Gospel

A cross
with four arms (two
century's growth) spiked up
in that witch's yard overnight—
cactus

thief!—we
all knew it. We
christened him *Verde*, watched
him tremble as if struggling to
breathe. We

witnessed
bellows ripple,
heave—the rubbery flesh
between ribs cracking at dusk like
our car's

sun-baked
vinyl seats. With
black lights we watched skin split,
scorpions spilling brightly from
Verde's

torn side.
And some of these,
freed from winter's slumber,
tumbled numbly to the ground, while
others

were snatched
mid-fall by bats—
blue-green, pincer-pronged stars
streaking through the clear night air like
wishes.

Dawn Manning

East Valley Nights

The desert's the least lonely place I know.
Coyote's voice carries for miles—
trick that quivers the spines of saguaros
unfolding down South Mountain to
the rumpled shawl of foothills flicker-fringed
by streetlamps weaving amber streaks
into the weft of suburban sprawl. No one
watches moonlight lap the salt from
dry riverbeds alone. I believe in
the mirage, there on the far side
of the valley, where the highest lanterns
of earth marry the lowest lights
of heaven—a pointillist universe
that undivides you and me from the stars.

Dawn Manning

Turquoise Inlay

The Easter after his liver transplant,
Freddie and his pickup make the pilgrimage to
Santuario de Chimayo
Behind other believers
Who have witnessed
Wheelchairs, walkers, and eyeglasses
Abandoned against adobe walls.

This Resurrection Sunday,
Diligent droplets like miniature suns
Gaze at the sacred hole.
Freddie remembers it from high school:

Then
—As deep and wide and broad as his Eagle football helmet;

Now
(In his sixtieth year),
—As deep and wide and broad as his Eagle football helmet,

Still.

He lowers his sack and scoops his soil.
Amongst clumps, clods, and God-shaped grains,
A turquoise stone stows away,
The same shade of dazzling sky
Lingering above Sangre de Cristo.

Linda Maxwell

Camping on Navajo Lake

The wind bruised the air blue
and the moon was not yet up
to where in the sky it could make a difference
to an observer trying to penetrate the dark.

Night things communicate a cryptic cacophony
that chills to the bone's marrow—
a clamorous equation piercing the ear to leave the mind
open to the exclamations but closed to their meaning.

Soaking under starlight the lake is diamond-dusted
and the shore a silent raven at midnight.
With only the moon to measure progress time seems
briefly inactive and the Earth suspended in its whirl.

Bray McDonald

Dusk with Forest Fire

We wake, if we ever wake at all, to mystery, rumors of death,
beauty, violence . . .

~ Annie Dillard

We are standing at the edge
of complete dark, the forest
burning as harbinger
of greater conflagration,
where the water that would baptize
us turns chemical-fetid, even
the rocks screaming pain-to-come.

But you insist we sing thanks
into the flames and dying ponds,
toward mountains of granite
and schist, quartz and eternity,
even toward the looming darkness.

Thanks for the falling light,
the smoke-battered moon sailing
nonchalant toward places
we have never seen, the wounds
that, on bad days, are all we have
to tell us we are here at all. The choir
of birds and coyotes and the earth
turning, its basso rumble rolling
through us, to wake us.

Thanks for the last stand
with our hands touching, our
hearts in that metaphorical
way poets hate to mention
for fear of exposure, the benevolence
of chance that rings up a life.
This life in the cold and heat,
the wind rising and falling and then . . .

We sing thanks for time, transience
accepted as beauty under our singular
breastbone, for the music born of it. Blues
and Bach and an old man playing spoons.
Sing words that never quite reach
but strain and turn and continually transform—
by this flickering light—with the effort.

Michael McIrvin

Poem for the True Earth

. . . mind is no other than mountains and rivers
and the great wide earth, the sun and the moon and the stars.

~ Dōgen

I wanted to write a poem
to equal the sky, starlight
and moon shadow giving way
to frosted sun.

I wanted to map the interior
of a stone, to coin a word
for that utter dark untouched
by light a million years,
a word for an ache hard and deep.

I wanted to be the air
through an owl's primaries,
the salience of talons, the poetry
of a field mouse's last sigh
as it dangles in low dawn.

I wanted to write the wind up,
a variable wind so the music
might be complex, a stout-hearted
blast filled with menace one minute,
caressing you with favor the next.

I wanted to write a poem
to equal the true earth. Not
the lazy version in the imagination
but the sharp edge where the mind
recognizes itself at last.

The poem of the fox
in the windrow, her perfect
gaze that captures everything,
moving and still. The poem
of the rabbit, the tick tasting the rabbit.

A poem of blood riding the rising light.
The negative charge of my heartbeat.
The positive charge of yours. The sky
deep as all thought, wide as prayer.

Michael McIrvin

Gallo Campground, September 8

Dusk has darkened canyon walls.
The thinnest seam of light traces

the eastmost bluff—nothing more
and then a mild glow, ivoried slip of sky

gently arcing, edgeless petal unfolding
into a perfect full moon bathing

Chaco Canyon's wide expanse in gleam
and shadow. Here, with distance—

with millennia of timeless rock
and crumbling walls—silence sequesters us

from depredations run amok elsewhere.
Here—while this miraculous light

washes the canyon walls, moonglow
enters us. Here—it is almost possible to believe.

David Meischen

Along the Turquoise Trail Byway

I smell secret notes. Desert rain and piñon. When I come home at twilight,
I wash clothes and pin them on a laundry line with bedsheets. I want
comfort: my neighbor's red chile enchiladas, an empty ashtray, and cheap
scotch. I want morning as warm and spicy, burnt cinnamon, to recover
from the accident. I swore after the bone crunch. My Honda hit a javelina.
Grizzled black and grayish hair, tailor-built suit, coarse enough to navigate
thorny cactus spines but no longer bristling. Hind feet with fused dewclaw.
At the neck, a white collar like a necklace I yanked to drag its body
from the undercarriage to beyond the byway's white-striped, thin shoulder.
A musk perfume as nervous as what's leftover as a remainder. Or a reminder?
Being alive is an act becoming too quick and messy. I'm a guilty humanoid.
Now, I want to climb a mountain in the background to recover. I wear hope,
a snow cap I never want to take off.

John Milkereit

For the Bats That Flew at Me Exiting the Carlsbad Caverns

after Hanif Abdurraqib

Sweethearts, if your evening exodus is normally now / I will accept this departure / but how do you know when sunset is? / I am not from here, unfamiliar / the park's *odorscape* / the aroma of algerita / the acrid smell of cave swallows / entrance scent is not you / I found out later / your perfume is notorious, deeper inside / I would prefer not to enter / I can't convince myself / I was a pup once / hanging together with brothers / mother swooping in / opening doors of our darkened rooms / to check if our noses were clean / not hanging from the ceiling / but your room is better / an outdoor amphitheater / tonight, a band of teal-colored sky / radiant yellow sunset / oncoming deep blue nightfall / to be caught into / I am sorry / you actually *fluttered over* / how adulthood is captured flight from myth / of unknown tribes / listen, sweethearts / I squint to admire / tiny leathery wings / sharp angles / I love your break over the horizon / zoom the dim light / if only you'll return / I will not beg for another flyover / if only to hold you / I offer an apology / I welcome future clicks and squeaks / to know where I am / my moodiness is no summer rodeo / but galloped away / migrating to a location where? / a sweet mystery.

John Milkereit

Gravity Is All There Is

The Tucson spring fills my car through open windows, small
hallelujahs of doves swell in the air, and you are driving. Golden
dust rises to warm our palms—your left, my right reaching out
toward cholla spines glowing at sunset on both sides of the road.

This is why my hands ache. Unable to touch, to turn
the truth of you into simple matter. Lit by sun, the blond hair
on your arm next to mine is an aura, but what pulls
is the solidity of your wrist, its drum, its weight.

I am not afraid you are all I have. I can hear the difference
between wanting to root and the carnal command of gravity.
My body accepts being tied to this wild it lives in. Like what's taut
between eight legs beating to the thrum of tarantula wasp.

This is the kind of love I love you with.
Can you fall down on me as plainly as you do onto clean sheets
at midnight after strumming for strangers? Even though
you no longer want to yield to the tug of my pulse,

even though you want your fingers free from anything
stronger than the briefest attachment—
if now all you will hold long enough is the steering wheel,
faded grave flowers, rocks and well-worn picks,

then talk.
And sing.
Give me the skin of your voice to wrap around what I want
to be bound to. That is all I can carry in this heat.

Michele M Miller

All Things Now Remind Me of What Love Used to Be

That small graveyard south of here, its anonymous dead tamped
down under impossibly high stacks of stones, plastic flowers, mangy,
bereft of color. Clustered in the dark, slurred over rusted crosses,
lambent voices I truss into conversations I'm sure I've had. Or wish
I'd have. Easy miracles: the blare of a match, its death as my breath
urns to smoke, water at last leaping from the broken tap, coyotes
raucous in the side yard yipping over a rabbit hot with blood,
me able to fall asleep. The past. The past is this:

to be innocent of the inevitable. It's the *not-knowing*
that happiness can only be had when want is wrenched
from dread and conjecture and every honeyed memento.
Only after the body comes clean.

Michele M Miller

One Dusk at White Sands

Near Alamogordo, dunes of gypsum thwart
The sun's capacity in starkest glare
Of day. Sky dome shifts dark. Grand palettes court
A dozen mates by end of western flare.
This dying of the sunlight sparks a hymn,
An anthem strummed upon our backs. We touch,
Our sense of heat intensified. Our spirits brim
With greater awe of stars more out of reach.
And then a lusty eastern globe appears,
To lasso our attention with its gaze
Of feigned surprise. Oh, barren Luna, hear
In sand-strung heartbeats Earth's primeval praise
For lovers. Fingers locked enthrall Moon's face;
Beyond our pull, cold orbs make love to space.

Judith Austin Mills

Sitting in a Stuffed Chair at the Edge of a Ravine

I am a bother to the birds
this early morning though
I try to stay still, only the pen
moving across a page, only my hand

raising and lowering a coffee cup
to the no-kill rodent trap
positioned like an end table
at my right, its mouth closed,

no one inside. I can't prevent
my eyes' flicking from sugarbush
to scrub oak to rosemary decked out
in purple flowers and the golden

radiance of bees. White-crowned
sparrows mob a lemonade berry bush,
argue uproariously, late on
their migration north,

quail call from a hillside
then run silently up a path,
goldfinches give their two-note
whistles up-down down-up,

even a thrasher, shyest of birds,
flits near my feet, carries
his scimitar beak
into the undergrowth.

A brown towhee diligently
checks and rechecks
the crumbling picnic table
for seeds and insects,

ravens circle through blue,
a roadrunner flies to the apex of a roof
to scout for lizards or a mate,
gives a throaty six-times *hoo*.

Penelope Moffet

Sunrise in Canyonlands

The cool morning sky is still awash with pulsating, salt-glazed starlight. At Mesa Arch, we find Orion, search for Pegasus, trace the Milky Way's scrawl across the darkness. For a few moments, we believe that this boundless space is meant for us; that its endless time is our endless time.

The stars retreat as the sky brightens, gradually shedding shards of time. The sun, our own relentless timekeeper, is arriving to set us straight, to teach us the language of time. Now we see our forgotten boundaries: the canyons that spread below us, the horizons that surround us, the thin swipe of atmosphere that envelops us.

We begin to understand. The sun drums the slow rhythm of time: Days, months, years. Lifetimes. Each with its own beginning and ending. We learn this lesson as the sun rises: A day unfurls before us; eternity is behind us.

Gayle Moran

One Great Love

I have drawn the curtains
on this little beating heart
of a cabin;

soaked in silence
in the double-slipper clawed tub;

communed with the orange tongue
in the arched mouth of the fireplace.

Outside, the river is endless.
Stunning stars tiptoe
around the moon;

and somewhere,
in that black pearl of night
is you.

karla k. morton

Easter Morning on the Way to Nevada Great Basin

She wondered
if she was called to these National Parks
like her friend Margaret is called to pray—

prayer, that one thing we all can do
from our easy chair,
our hard pew,
our rug in the eastern sun.

She thought of Johnny Appleseed,
John Muir,
the twelve disciples,
Meriwether Lewis.

She thought of the way her life
became something greater
when she knelt
and felt Old Faithful's ancient waters,
or witnessed sunrise on Cadillac Mountain,

or felt the saguaro's cool green skin—
the way she'd touched it
between the spines,
and traced the holes in its
early dawn body

like Mary must have done,
when Jesus appeared
Easter morning.

She remembered peering into
the round wound of the cactus,

the tiny flutter of the bird
taking sanctuary;
the way she knew
every feather on its head
was counted.

karla k. morton

Into the Night

after Peggy McGivern's painting, named in this poem's title,
Jones Walker Gallery, Taos, New Mexico

As soon as mother shut the door
I sprang up barefoot onto the cold tile floor and ran
to the window. I whistled and called until
you galloped to the sill—your glistening red
coat scented with sage, majesty radiating
from your antlers—that breath-stealing rack
of male-hood -wild-pronged splendor
that reared back in greeting as I leapt down
into the hot curve of your spine, my fingers
gripping your fur, my white chemise
billowing behind me like angel wings.
We tore into that immense black mouth
of night that had swallowed all the stars.
Violet hills cradled us between their thighs.
Grass sizzled beneath your hooves, our hearts
thundered as one, drumming our way to freedom.

Ruth Mota

Sweet Pea

At daybreak, she wanders through sweet peas
growing wild by the Jemez River
She eats the pods—
ignores those who say these vines are weeds.
What do they know about the vigorous elegance that fills her mouth?

The green lime of cottonwood leaves holds the morning
and he wades towards her
his bare feet gingerly stepping into the cold, rushing water.

The clouds move on near the mesa cliffs
and they remark about the heady ephedra—
its whorled nodes of green branchlets camouflage
their petty arguments,
rise up to their quietly whispered affections.

They plant some in their garden,
take back their wildness.

> *Jules Nyquist*

Cusp

That point where the stonework reaches the ceiling
       defines the tangent
of the hacienda fireplace at dusk

A crescent of guests on Día de Los Muertos
       gathers around the hearth—
the architecture of an arch

The living descendants feed the fire with their chatter—
       offering sheets of words
to leave invisible ink in their mouths

Paper-thin talk of orders left behind
       ignite last testaments
in a quiet cauldron of siege

Flames fill the room
       with shadows
that soften the war stories

The alcohol amplifies the voices
       as flames cackle and spit—
tallow candles drip their wax into pools of grief

In the kitchen
       the blue pilot light of the stove
burns to sustain the holy

Volatile flames sputter as oxygen leaves the room
       embedded wicks are drawn down
cupping the throbbing earth

Outside, the frost on the dirt
        is a sealing wax—
a letter of truce

A comet shoots across the sky
        as if
it could rewrite everything

Jules Nyquist

Wild Nights

The sphinx moth hovers in the mouth
of the moonflower, its throat glowing

like a candle to lure her to its pools
of hallucinogenic nectar. Her tongue,

one of the longest of all insect species,
uncoils deep into its fragrant channel

as its stamens brush her legs and wings
with pollen to carry to another's pistil.

They have been at this for a long time,
evolved to practice their nocturnal trysts

and acts of "accidental" pollination.
Unaware, we imagine they are unaware

of the seductive arts and manipulation
they're drawn to perform under cover

of darkness. Well, there is that cactus moth
who fastens a wad of pollen onto the stigma

of its beloved flowers to farm fresh food
for its caterpillars in the Arizona desert.

Far older species than we, love, they know
full well the nature of wild! Wild nights—

Katherine Durham Oldmixon Garza

Our Little Life

In the widow's hour, you awaken
me with the flutter of your hands

on bongos. I stir, turn to where you
must be beside me, listen to Tish

sing, "Tu Que Puedes, Vuelvete."
It's not a dream. Your iPad is playing

Aquella Noche.
                              Not a dream,
I say, staring into the dark, out

our dark window. If I were asleep,
I could see you, touch you, hear you,

like the time we were driving down
to see your mother, a jar of cactus blooms

in the cupholder, or when you took me
to a house of glass and light over the Gulf,

or came in another body, a mountain
lion offering a riddle about honey

and time. In a dream, my mortal senses
know we are together. How our life

is rounded by a sleep—I close my eyes
to listen, let myself sink under the weight

of your absence in our bed. To sleep,
so perchance you will return; return

if you can, before the diurnal sun
blurs my vision, parts our life again.

Katherine Durham Oldmixon Garza

Rendezvous

Night falls slowly, as it does in summer, when the air is clear and not dark with rain. For when the rain comes over, across, and down off the mountains, the aspen tremble and quake in the gray sky as the winds push the weather into the valley and no one can tell when slate-gray day, with its streaks of blue corn gray and mottling of flint and graphite, deepens into the charcoal and then onyx of night. But when the sky is clear and the sun moves behind the ridgeline and its light lines the darkening mountains in silver, the sky stays a clear, limpid, starless blue for hours as the air cools and the high chirp and trill of the larks, sparrows, wrens, and tanagers we did not hear in the heat of the day returns to float above the boreal chorus of frogs and the sound of the river swollen with snowmelt, rushing over rock. They say the stars near Angel Fire are a wonder, but the moon has risen full and orange. And so it is. We set out for the thing we think we want the most, a river of light flowing through a darkened sky, but are given, instead, something else:

> strawberry moon
> a large heliodor
> shining through the pines

Jeremy Paden

Ruidoso

House wrens flit between the cabin porch and the stand of quaking aspen where ground squirrels poke their heads from burrow holes. The braver pups wrestle as adults stand guard or scurry across the lawn, their chatter barely heard above the morning song of sparrows. A donkey brays over by the barn. In the field, the blue and white wings of black-billed magpies skim above the grass. The dog chases robins the way that robins chase magpies, then squats in the stream because a clean dog that has fiercely kept the lawn bird-free is a happy dog in need of a good wallow. Above us, the blue and white and violet-green of swallows spin and slice through the air, unconcerned with dogs or robins. They, like us, have just arrived in the valley and are busy hunting for cavities in cabin roofs and tree trunks, as broad-tailed hummingbirds and calliopes buzz about the eaves and sip the sap left by woodpeckers.

> mountains
> make their own light
> feathery clouds turn pink

Jeremy Paden

Rising

Soft thunder. Rain trickles over the edges of the eaves and drops down the downspouts. The sky is silvery gray and the parlor lights are lit and warm. I sit with my purring laptop and my purring tailless tuxedo cat. My big coffee mug is empty. Outside the plate glass window, an old oak's branches release raindrops onto hot flagstones. A garden bell made of a halved propane tank hangs from the porch post, its Asian glyph reflects the invisible wings of a hummingbird's ghost.

Misha Penton

*The sun drums the slow rhythm of time: Days, months, years.
Lifetimes. Each with its own beginning and ending. We learn this
lesson as the sun rises: A day unfurls before us; eternity is behind us.*

Gayle Moran

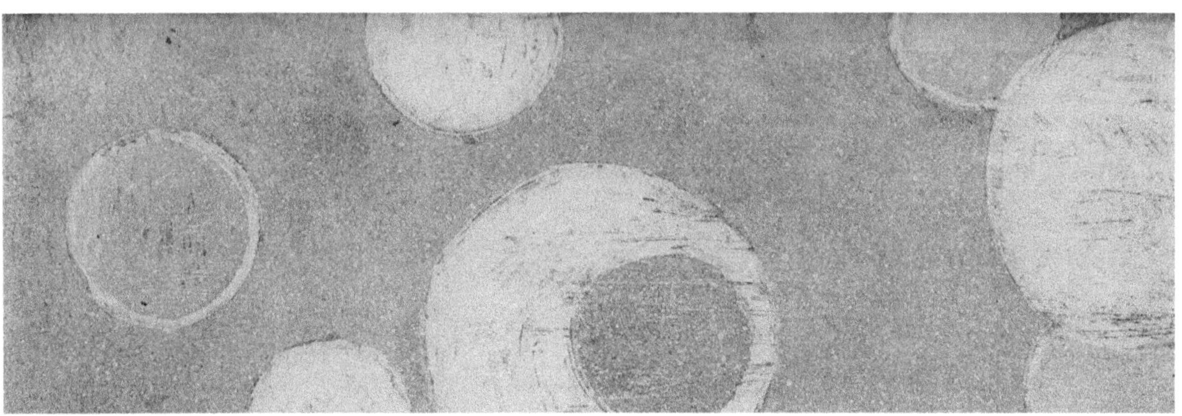

Light Enough

I step into the end
of night. The porch light
catches my breath, holds
it tight in the winter air.
The only sign I'm warm-
blooded. I inhale resolve.

I run right away into the dark,
follow the streetlights,
anchored constellations
aligned in simple terms.
The sun rises slowly,
a quiet, polite gesture.

The moon lingers
wrapped in a silence
only sleep can bring.
Each mile, I notice the sky's
subtle shift, as my legs
remember their purpose:

warm muscles moving bones.
I pass houses holding
still, blanketed bodies.
My lungs take in the cold
without complaint.

At the park I circle
before heading back, I hear
the call of a Cooper's hawk,
its repeated short address.
My ears search for the sound
in the surrounding oaks.

The sky holds just enough
blue of the day to come.
The leafless trees stretch
and flatten against it in pure
silhouette.

I can even make out
the thinnest branches,
each line of reasoning
and change of heart,
everything trees can hide
in warmer, greener seasons.

And it's just light enough
to spot the alert bird perched
high on an inner branch. Just
light enough to prove the end
of night's tunnel. I run on.

Jennifer Frank Pontzer

Descend into Dark

Two owls to the tree by the flow
descend in the dark, shadow
of the moon's bright mark
on the canyon of the Gila, slow,
lighting on branches, clutching bark,
far from the cities of men.

Here tents and hikers once stood,
too confident to comprehend
that time is cottonwood.

Too young and unafraid
of how the river's flow can braid
time's woven noose in riverbeds,
"Descend in the dark," they said.

They had walked the hills in daylight,
thought they would keep to the trail
of friendship beyond this night.
Their hopes would someday fail.

Before the canyon's stark
walls, in shadow and light
from the moon's watermark,
the men argue good and right
as two owls descend into dark,
oracles of Minerva flying
from sunset into thickets, crying
to the young and unafraid,

"Strike, for then it's gone
and done." For all their trying
to see beyond the dawn,
their fate is not yet made.

Frank Pool

Facing Up

The San Juans still had icepack in July, and I drank from the living waters of a spring, and I looked up and saw the Milky Way stretching across the sky-dome its brightness and shocking darknesses I had never ever seen, and I saw light and dark and dust and gravity and no life anywhere in that lifeless light and dark, light and heavy, all atoms and the void, and I knew a fear that stopped at nothing.

Tonight would freeze this high sky ridge of stone and skinny lodgepole pines, and I would linger still, looking across time and distance, light years across the lighted ecliptic, order and chaos, creation and destruction, looking for something alive besides me and you and us and them, and the light lit large sky is still and silent as the galaxy rotates in its deep and shining time.

Just then it all swept inside me, immanent and merciless, in the coolness of my breath, as I stood facing up to it.

Frank Pool

The day after I die

two deer come up from the creek—
are they surprised
that I'm not on the path?
surprised
that they didn't catch me
off-guard
as they crashed through the willows?
Will they look for me
as I did for them
on these late summer mornings?
Probably not.

But isn't that the way it should be?

Despite my absence
the day unfolds
like it did yesterday
        —the red-tail hawk swoops at the darting rabbit—
like it will tomorrow
        —the creek ripples over the smooth rock.
Things move forward.

Oh, I'm certain I will be missed
maybe intensely at first—
others surprised at my absence—
then less so as time goes on.
A faint fragrance
hangs in the air—
ponderosa pine in the damp morning—
the last note of a song,
the brush stroke of watercolor
soaking into paper.

Two deer will come up from the creek.

I may be remembered
when the leaves
start their change
from summer green to fall gold
and aspen leaves quiver,
quake, in the morning breeze
as it all stretches out, even
the day after I die.

Vince Puzick

Nightlock

All the losses gather
like birds
who no longer
know how to winter.

Earth alone is a stone
not feeling itself,
not recognizing
its moltenness
that in any case
has cooled and hardened
beyond reckoning.

No one expects
warmth or welcome.

Singing does not
catapult a response.

So we migrate
to ourselves
and gather separately
among the howling

hills, these skeletons
who know well
the emptiness
arriving with wind.

David Radavich

Stone Fruit

The first perfectly ripe peach of summer,
delicate flesh melting on my tongue,

sweet fragrance mixed with
the acidity of memory—my mother

alone at the breakfast table,
barely dawn and already

Dad's shirts on the line and row after row
of Ball jars packed tight with perfect peach halves.

Dust blows off the desert, a gray shroud
softening the sunrise.

Why did I come back so late, after memory had failed her
and she barely knew my name?

I think of her in quiet moments alone
as I eat my peaches with a slice of toast.

She preferred the taste of clings
but always canned the freestones.

Morgan Ray

Memory Triggered by a Late Snowfall in March

after Michael Lavers

Trees, streets, and parked cars outside my window. White trees, and white streets and white cars, and birds, and beyond that, snowy mountains. The sun rises over the mountains and the streetlights begin to flicker. Parting clouds glow pink. Downspouts trickle. A squirrel sits on a branch, tail in the air, eyeing the Brazil nuts I set out last night, now cotton-covered lumps. And, yes, I also see in my mind that pristine March day when a vested man at King Soopers pulled an AR-15 and the woman with the shopping cart ran but had no voice to scream, apples spilling, as her unpiloted cart rolled across the parking lot. Next, a plumber fled for his van and inside the store, a girl cowered in the cereal aisle holding up a pleading hand. Who can explain to me why this happened? Wrong place? Wrong time? Random act? It's spring and there are trees, side-walks and cars covered with snow. The melt is rapid, the sunrise brilliant and my misplaced joy at this glimmering sight knows this is not the end of mass shootings in my life. Part of me has accepted the senselessness and no longer seeks justice, which is impossible anyway. But, I will not forget Uvalde, Parkland, Paradise and all the rest. First one, then three, then more than I can count. The trees are shedding snow and this cascade is glorious. I step outside, listen to the muffled thuds as clumps of snow hit the ground and, for a moment, bask in this unstained landscape.

Morgan Ray

Matins Without Hummingbirds

First I check the nest, though they're long gone.
The birds were not my children, but they grew
in the shadow of my house, buzzing my lawn
& sipping from my catmint. Then they flew.
Mere weeks, but long enough to get attached
to the pattern of my early morning visit:
just the two of us, before the nestlings hatched—
two watchwomen, anxieties implicit
& greater once the twins entered the fray,
their épées flailing gaily, safety-edged.
Another week, & then a pink-cheeked day:
the braver took one final feeding, fledged.
The second perched an hour, piqued & thrumming,
then tossed itself to what was always coming.

Erica Reid

The Ceremony

a blue jay
flits about
shooting star

We don our hiking boots and head up the hill outside your house. You hold my hand to steady me on the steepest part of the incline. We're on the way to our wedding.

It's a second marriage for each of us. We both like to keep things simple. No minister, no traditional vows, and no guests. We sit down on a massive boulder high above the city. A breeze ruffles your auburn hair.

For a while we just hold hands and watch as streaks of pink, red, and orange spread their fingers across the evening sky like a jet trail. Then you play "The Rose" on your harmonica; I read a poem I've written. The rest is silence.

the dream house
you built on the mesa
two cats in the yard

Sharon Rhutasel Jones

Dawn Patrol

A single hot-air balloon
glides gently
at daybreak
above the bosque's cottonwoods
low enough to see
a motionless canoe
in the river

The Río Grande runs
north to south
in New Mexico
so crossing it does not lead
to freedom
or opportunity

Only the momentary joy
of this perfect autumn morning
suspended between heaven and earth
in an envelope of stillness
and a peace
you'd swear
encompassed the globe

John Roche

Disturbed Pastoral

begins with rose light we sleep through
wake to seamlessness   white cloth settled
as if readying a summer feast

but it is not summer
nor is there food to feed the length of a trestle table

By feed I mean   we are hungry
snow its own miracle of manna

Though look   already the dog
has spoiled it   so now allow
the sharp-shinned hawk

to tear prey from a low limb
press into white earth
the captured robin

Surely the hawk has punctured the breast
Wind unsettles his back   He does not look up

I cannot see how hard the talons work
or hear a death wheeze or feel
melting beneath

Then it is over
The hawk lifts   swerves   carries its kill

Evidence is delicate   a trail of blood stains
soft feathers like grass   ice-caught and wind-torn

And there   look
the whole tail   a fan
spread so I can study every overlap

every hue   how rust merges into black
black to gray   how each narrowing white tip
disappears against snow

    Barbara Rockman

Desert Fever

The fever of the desert night still burns in my blood, your body melting into mine like wildfire through sage. My hands still hold your ghost beneath the silver light of New Mexico's moon bleeding mercury through dreams that never break, never fade, this endless burning, the taste of you still desert-wild on my breath.

Even alone I'm scorched by your phantom breath, lightning crackling electric through my blood. When I shift these blankets rough as sage, still burning for the vision of you moving through the sage and chaparral like smoke, disrupting dreams, mi corazón, you blaze brighter than moonlight.

Pueblo fires can't match your inner light. Cedar smoke can't cleanse the fever of your breath from my lungs, where you live in waking dreams and sleeping visions, poison in my blood sweet as desert honey, wild as sage in summer storms, forever burning.

When dawn comes over mesas, still burning with the memory of your touch, morning light reveals the world unchanged: ocotillo, sage, the same thin air that holds your phantom breath, the same red earth that calls to restless blood, the same endless sky that cradles dreams.

If I could trade a lifetime of these dreams for one more night of fever, bodies burning together in the darkness, pulse and blood and breath entwined beneath that silver light—but you are gone, and I am left with breath that tastes of loss and longing, bitter sage.

The high desert keeps its secrets: wind through sage, coyote songs, the architecture of dreams built from moonbeams and the ghost of your breath. All night the sacred fires keep burning while I lie awake in pools of silver light, desert fever pulsing through my blood.

Through sage and dreams your phantom breath keeps burning. In silver light my restless blood runs wild. This fever burns eternal in the sage, in dreams, in breath, in blood, in burning light.

Aroma Rodrigues

We set out for the thing we think we want the most,
a river of light flowing through a darkened sky . . .

Jeremy Paden

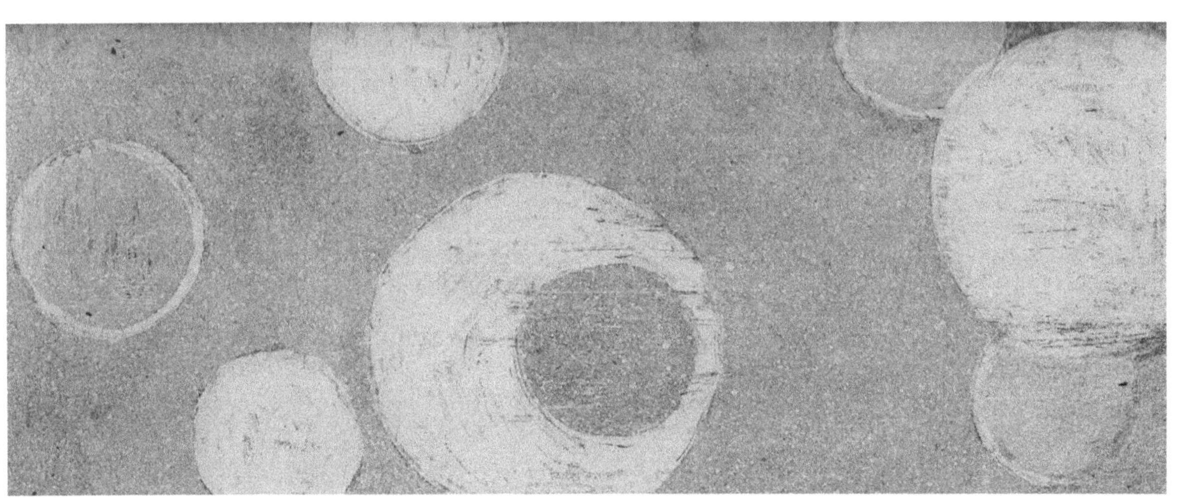

Mountain Strangeness

First night in Winter Park.
Long past midnight,

you lie awake.
Traces of aspen, pine
cool your breath.

Taut with mountain,
quivers of sound
prickle the air, your skin.
A chill breeze

disturbs the trees. Critters
rustle in the dark. Eyes

taste the texture of night,
imagine shadows,
silent wings.

Toward dawn,
silhouettes. Swallows
chitter through columns of dark,
fading with the unexpected

moan of a train.
                        Clatter and throb

choke the sounds of mountain,
leaving only

the voiceless crying of steel,
frosty ringing.
Echoes off the mountain

linger, caught
in branch and rock,

bone.

Gary S. Rosin

El Nogal Trail at Sunrise

In the distance
road rumbles its echoing
reverberations.

The climb, green lichen dusted.
I suck wind while scrub oak
crinkles.

Crow soars in annoyance.
We've disturbed her roost
amid the piñon.

Along the keystone laid path
it's clear we are not the first.
Scuffed tread and elk pellets—

a Hansel and Gretel mark
that will dissipate and
erode toward clusters of paddle cactus.

Those spines reveal a toughness
I have learned to keep close.
Why is it so easy to be a black sheep?

Lookout met—
legs dangle over precipice.
Taos greets us through the haze.

The going down
is a knee-trembling
relief.

Shelli Rottschafer

At Day's Break: Sapphic Stanzas

Singe me an incendiary wind song.
Ashen boughs pine for gray dove flight.
Wile-weaving limbs twine a matrix
> of bittersweet love.

Iris seeks apertured opening.
Moon's curves crescent-shape
her sculpture spoons, but
> my thoughts sleep alone.

A cacophony of ravens
Sing their prize
And beat their wings as if
> to embrace, daybreak.

Shelli Rottschafer

Falling

golden shovel series after haiku by Buson, Chiyo-ni and Bashō respectively

I.

Startled awake in the
night, I see the bright boat of spring
rocking gently on a sparkling sea.
Rubbing my eyes and rising,

I stumble to the window and
see the fiery trail of a falling
star, and the waxing moon rising

over the mountains. I am awake and
dreaming at the same time, falling
into an equinox reverie where all
the world teeters between night and day.

II.

It is not the having,
but the discovering—last evening I gazed
from my chair on the back porch at
watermelon mountains in the
afterglow. Suddenly the full moon

burst from the crest like a milky marble and I
had to remember to breathe. I will not depart
this world without the image from
such a bedazzled night. Or this—
the opalescent gleam of datura blooms. Life

is sweet for hawkmoths drinking moonlight with
an enthusiasm of ecstasy. I tell you a
secret—the simplest things can be a blessing.

III.

The sun is going down on
September, golden leaves twist in a
sultry breeze, then fall, lay bare
the gnarled cottonwood branch.

A bright bed below. In this leaving, a
shadow and its wings descend—the crow
ruffles her feathers as she lands,

a reminder of what follows autumn—
the dark plumage of a winter dusk.

    Janet Ruth

As Long As It Lasts

. . . I sang the best songs that were sung in the world
as long as a song lasts . . .

~ W.S. Merwin, "Peire Vidal"

the cool caress of down-canyon breeze at dusk
last scratch on the page when the pen runs out of ink
on my tongue, remnant fire after a bowl of green chile stew
glow from the last ember on the hearth
whisper of a cricket below my window
the *amen* of a canyon wren's song in San Ignacio's tower

before the orchestra is tuned, the tuning fork's vibration
the last reverberation of a cello string
glitter from one last star just before dawn
lingering sweetness from the datura bloom's silver trumpet
the shimmer of mountains in a desert mirage
after the pond's cacophony, a final spadefoot murmur

the last drop of water on the tongue
shadows of clouds dragging across the mesa
before lightning, the smell of ozone
a grumble of thunder after the flash
the scent of petrichor after the rain
rumble in a dry arroyo just before the wall of water

and at the end, that is just another beginning . . .
taste of water from a melting glacier
the last view of this wild and awe-full world
as they close my eyes, the gentle touch of fingers
glimmer of fireflies   or velvet darkness
or music   or what comes next?

musk of molecules splitting and merging in the alchemy of rot
the whisper of a feather lifting on the air
becoming invisible
fragments
            of memory
                    drift
    in an abandoned
                        house

Janet Ruth

Watching for Meteors

A frigid night—down coat zipped tight—shiver and pray
for one glimpse of a falling star, just fleetingly,
as it burns out—from flame to cinder in the sky.
But the illumination of the full moon's glow
makes me wonder if its bright will obscure my view
of lesser lights, and so my faith is tried, it's true.
In the slightly darker spot cast by the smoke tree's shadow,
the wait for ancient rocks from constellation Gemini.
Then, having given up all chilly hopes, I see
one brilliant flair arc across heaven, fade away.

Janet Ruth

Gathering dark unravels our fears in silent swoon beneath bruised skies

Marcial Delgado

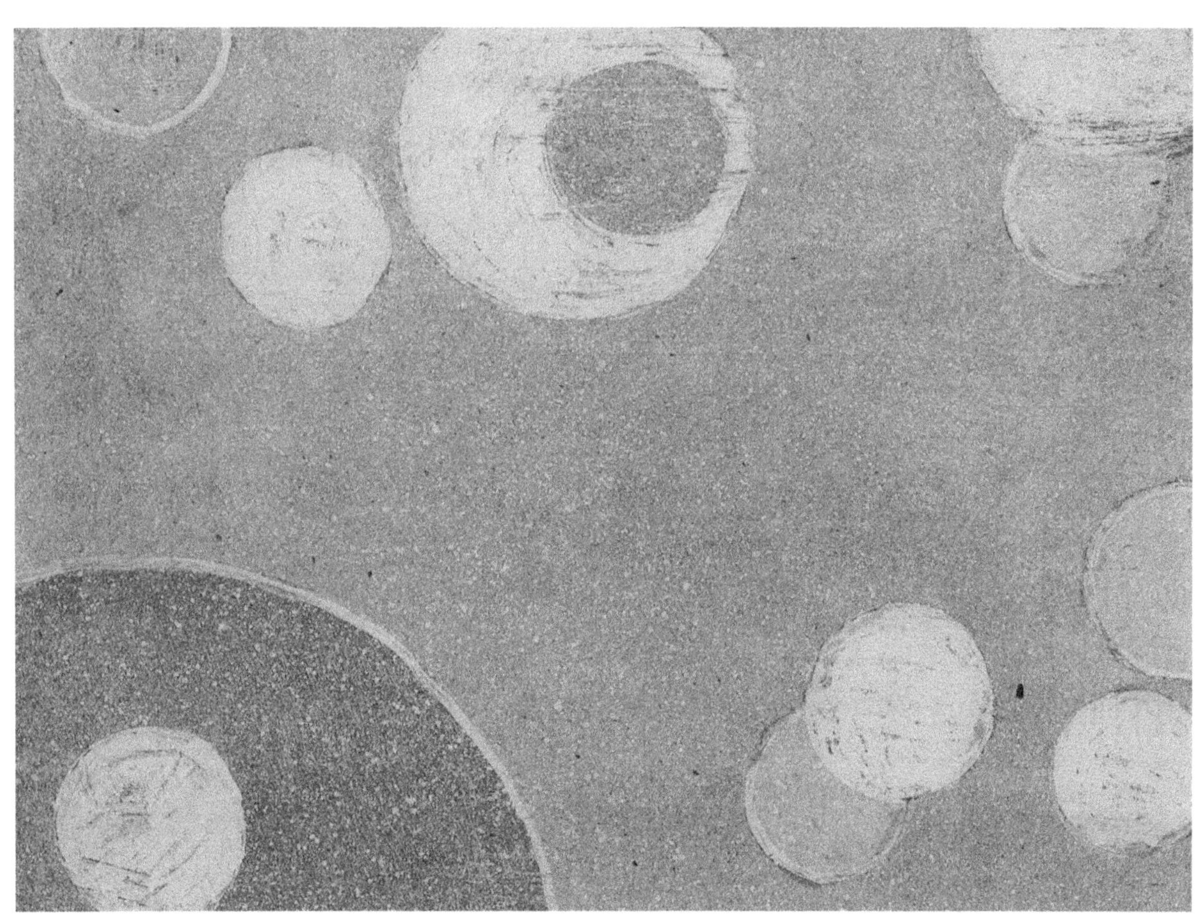

the whole rainbow of it

Moon is new tonight,
sky dark as silence
save for starlight.

A crescent proof of life
signals she is still
making her rounds,

waxing toward full.
In my mind's eye,
I see prickly pears

tumbling through barbed wire
on either side of the road,
Boer goats huddled in masses.

But my embodied eyes see nothing
more than a yellow stripe
to mark the middle

and a narrow swath of road
visible in the headlights
on the way to Amarillo.

Stars are points of light,
but starlight makes nothing
but nothing visible.

Night contains its own light
plus all the light
that glances off day,

the whole rainbow of it
ready to burst when
moon is full

two weeks further on.
When I see her
bright as the sun

in the corner of my eye,
I bow my head
and think of home.

Steven Schroeder

in this climate

Matins begins with birdsong before dawn.
Mist ascends from sprinklers on the clock in
close cropped lawns of children of immigrants
and children of children of immigrants
tended by immigrants and children
of immigrants and children of children
of immigrants mindful in this climate
of ice that should have melted long ago.
Mockingbirds make a joyful noise composed
of every sound they've ever heard.

Every one of them sounds like a rainbow
of birds. Bluejays squabble with squirrels
over peanuts and seeds in the birdfeeder
sister Susan filled religiously, a prayer
in her daily office. They scatter as many
as they eat. Some seeds fall on stone, where
grackles bow and scrape and take them all
as outward and visible signs
of inward and spiritual grace.
Some fall on soil hard as stone
to strut and fret and wither
like the gourd vine Jonah mourned.

Some fall on fertile ground, grow to bloom
a hundred flowers. Fog clings to earth, glows
with first light as thirsty sun slips over
the horizon to burn it off and blaze
so you'd think the whole world
was made of nothing but light.

Ravens fly to perches where
they can keep an eye on us,
take it all in, wonder who we
think we are, wonder what we
mean by we, wonder where we
will be when the water is gone.

Steven Schroeder

Por un amor perdido

Your breath: my breath
autumn sharp and clear.

Sunflowers stunted this year, no full
faced glory. A map

of mouse bones at our feet
and I tell you: I only want time.

Barter my place in line, polish the crystal ball.
Our answer not so certain.

Your skin: my skin
urge to possess, pull

my body from stone.
Is courage simply the willingness to return?

Kestrels clutter the treetops, cottonwoods
gossip: too late for another harvest.

The waning gibbous taunts me all night.
There may never be another song.

Katherine DiBella Seluja

Curtain Call

The sun, moon, and sky danced tonight.

You will have to take my word for it since
my phone fails as a camera in low light.

The moon looked like a drip of pink paint
on a shimmering pond, bleeding into waves
of white and purple, blue and green.

More Monet than Van Gogh, soft blurs, pastels,
dim impressions dimpled across the canvas
of the heavens and reflected in my eye.

Then, at that last moment, the sun broke
as it touched the tips of yucca on the brim
of the horizon, blistered spikes making one

final fling skyward, stoking fires in the clouds,
until black fell like a curtain, blanking the sky.

The dog and I hobbled home.

Audell Shelburne

Halfway There, and Scared

Walking after dusk, you get to know yourself.
The path to the cabin goes toward a night
so deep that its purple and navy swim
in your field of vision. Bright pinpoints—
lightning bugs—weave and turn before you.
Halfway there, and scared, you swing the lantern.
That is your habit to create a narrow path
through the swell of night. It drives you
forward even when you can't see, and in fear.
There's the awful pleasure of walking to get there
and trying not to make too much of the dark—
you won't be defined so much by it, or old losses.
This place doesn't tell that story. Up ahead
the covered porch takes form in soft yellow light.
There, you'll swat away the moths lively in it.

Rebecca A Spears

The Pause

The light comes up before the sun, and
morning pauses on the other side of the hill.

Night has already moved on,
leaving time and space briefly open,

offering the world a small,
dove-soft moment of quiet hope.

Doves flex and flap their wings.
An owl swoops through the mesquite
but no one hears it.

And now distant coyotes' voices
pierce the stillness, singing the sun up.

From the far side of the bed,
as from another country,
I hear you breathing.

Victoria Stefani

Fifth of May

Neo-plastic papel picado flutter
mango, papaya, and watermelon shine
in string-light luster for Cinco de Mayo.
I bare-throat a gulf-sized bowl of marisco,
overbite a lime rind mercy-drowned in beer.
Zinc-top's lacking dazzle pairs
to shoulders' clothesline-slack,
buttons frail, snap-catches flat.
Will stars be stereo tonight?
Will the moon, silver-sure, be one, or two?

With so many someplaces to be
I level north, conning directions
my feet don't yet know.

Prosser Stirling

Night Is a Mother

I believed in the tooth fairy without imagining what she looked like. All that mattered was whenever I left a baby tooth under my pillow, it would transform overnight into four quarters tucked in a handsewn fabric pouch. While it's too late to ask her, I suspect the tooth fairy was actually my mom. Only she could be so thoughtful, and she was a seamstress. Last night I dreamt of finding the cerulean gingham dress she made for me in third grade. A real tooth fairy would have been problematic. What kind of otherworldly ding-dong collects teeth? A ghoul who crunches on teeth for a 3 a.m. snack?

Some entity haunts our yard at night. It carries off mourning doves (O'odham: hoohi) that perished from illness, old age, or window strikes. We also live in the territory of a gray fox (O'odham: chuavi), so it is likely our dove fairy. Gray foxes are the size of cats, but stronger and nimbler. One summer night during a monsoon, lightning illuminated this desert fox leaping from branch to branch to the top of our pine tree until it vanished. I have never seen such supernatural grace. It's okay this omnivorous fairy doesn't leave coins in exchange for the doves. I imagine she is stitching together a home for her kits: a feather-soft house up high in the sky.

> transforming loss
> to solace
> quiet magic

Sharon Suzuki-Martinez

Earth Tone

In the nacreous,
watercolor wash
of twilight,

from the distant
pinprick
of vanishment,

a raven emerges
to sanctify
the vacuous sky

with plume, muscle
and the flutes
of hollow bones.

She showers
the darkening hues
of the desert

with the weightless,
crystalline screeches
of her cawing,

revving wide open
the bloody little
pistons of her heart.

Larry D. Thomas

Moon crushed to powder

I met you finally with the moon in the sky
cradled by purple clouds,
the moon crushed to powder,
bodies darkened beneath the orange canyon,
the fever of June approaching wildly.

Politely, you asked me to forget
everything before—
the sidewalks, the gray cities,
the house of mirrors,
the torturous winters,
the faces in the moon.

When I opened my eyes,
everything was gone but the taste
of your name in my mouth.

Shelby Tuthill

Of Horses and Hawks and All Things in Between

The morning sun is painting June
      on a blue-sky canvas
with slashing strokes of cirrus clouds
above the gathering greens of hickory
      and pecan trees,
guarding the eastern edge of pasture grass.

Another summer is being shaped
      in rising spirals
        of a redtail hawk
above a wicked twist of shallow river
where four horses emerge
from the mist along the muddy banks
as if being born
      from the earth itself.

This is my Oklahoma,
a locus of horse
      hawk
and all things that live between,
a painting
hung by a single strand
of antique barbed wire
on gnarled bois d'arc fence posts,
anchoring the world to the coming day.

Ron Wallace

I am not yet ready to rise,
not yet ready to push
away the romance of dreams
but invite morning
into the comfort of bed.

Elizabeth Black

Somewhere There's a Horse

The old man was sitting alone at the bar
         his back to me
at a Denny's restaurant
in Raton, New Mexico.
Tourists headed north for Colorado
         coming in for breakfast
paid him no more notice
than the pinon pines they'd just driven past.

He was built
thin and tough as a barbed wire fence.
His faded Levi blue jean jacket
         worn thin at the elbows
             looked like it came from 1962,
and his Wrangler jeans
were probably older than his waitress.
His cowboy hat,
a Stetson, I'm sure,
         once cream-colored
             now sweat-stained
was curled a little on one side
from too many years of pulling it down snug
against New Mexico winds.

I noticed the slight grimace
when he wavered
         for just a second
as he stepped down from his stool
seeking balance on the worn heels
         of his scuffed boots.

"Are you okay?"
the young waitress asked with true concern.
He nodded,
         "Just a little dizzy spell."

But as he turned
and placed a twenty-dollar bill
down on the bar
          I saw the look
              the silent pleading
                      in faded gray eyes
"No, not here.
Not in a goddamned Denny's."
He placed one foot
          slowly ahead of the next
just like a cowboy is supposed to do
and stepped out
into the cool Sangre de Cristo Mountain air,

where somewhere, I know, there was a horse.

Ron Wallace

Empty

A wolf moon
hangs in the January night sky
      indigo blue
with a scatter of stars spilling around it.

Outside
I stand below its light
in the ink-black shadow of trees
      shrouded in darkness,
no light from the darkened windows.

And I listen
listen for a single cricket's song
      or a coyote's howl,
maybe wind rattling the branches above,
but there is simply no sound
      only silence
         in an empty world.

Ron Wallace

Chaco Canyon, New Mexico, June 20, 2025

For Elizabeth

I.

Her memory shimmers, this dawn,
warms me as I hold each earring,
like a talisman in my hands
walking into the canyon.
Ancestral Pueblo people tracked the sun's
movement and lunar cycles: the universe explained
through signs, roads, seasons,
calling forward the faithful,
each in tune with the natural world.

II.

First light of the summer solstice
the Sand Dagger on Fajada Butte glistens, shafts of light
illuminate spiral petroglyphs carved into the rockface.
A dagger-shaped beam, a natural sundial
bisects the center of the spiral,
lifts, reaches beyond this world
where ancient astronomy and astrophysics
collide into the cyclical nature of the universe.

III.

From the soft flesh-pink of her helix
dangled Navajo earrings—
Mercury-dime silver, pounded,
polished into a spiral—
the cyclical nature of the universe
with her life's journey complete.
The warmth of silver on my face, in my hands—
inexplicable, mysterious, a thousand years later—
humbling, astonishing energy guiding
me through this vast planetary space.

Lynda Gerdin Webb

Between Time Zones

Perched atop the crumbling backdoor stoop
beneath an awning rusted by time & weather,

I'm out of earshot of my ill brother & mother,
gripping my cellphone, willing it to pulse.

Daybreak spills above conifers, elm & oak.
You're a thousand miles from Ohio in the Trans-Pecos

& an hour behind me, still asleep in the treasured
cobalt darkness of that desert region where telescopes

search galaxies billions of light years from Earth.
Our circadian rhythms have adapted to separation.

I rise at twilight, before another cycle of caretaking
quashes most chances to return, even briefly,

to you. If only our neighbor's rooster would crow
you awake. You'll groan, yawn, reach out & curse

that I'm gone, then prop yourself with pillows
& dial, knowing I find reassurance in your voice.

Marilyn Westfall

The Breath of Salvation

written after hearing Mr. Manygoats speak

Consider Charley Manygoats
who saw thirteen owls
the dawn after his conversion,
then stepped out into the cold
and opened his arms like wings,
preaching to them.

Frost like sin hung in the air
as owls curled talons
over branches, settled heavy heads
into shoulders older than rocks,
dark pinecones hung by witches
who nightly wooed the moon.

Seeing the glimmer
of sunlight on owls
Charley breathed the dawn,
chanted a prayer to morning,
whirled his songs of praise,
driving away the dark.

Janice Whittington

The Morning After

Scattered on the creek's edge
like dry leaves staining dirt red,
handprints of raccoons
who washed bits of worms
and patted mud,
tracks of turkeys running
splay-footed, hurried.

And on the bank,
deep prints of clawed pads,
proof of those night screams,
not the coyote's howl or bay
we sleep through, but
that shriek that draws us
into dreams of wildness,
a dark world
that snags us
in a taloned grip.

Janice Whittington

against curtains of night,
notes of light and dark.

Lucy Griffith

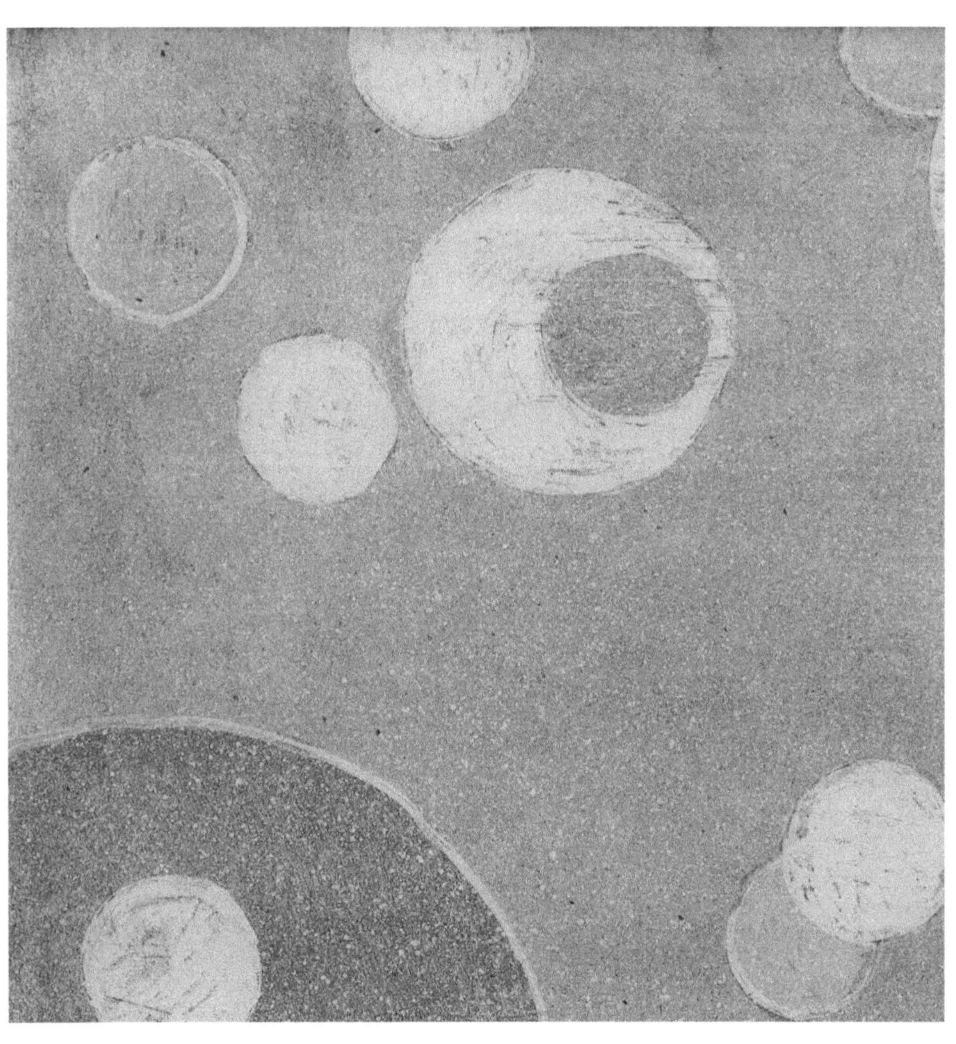

Somewhere in the Distance

Sky folds in on itself
over volcanoes to the west
in assorted cocktail hues.
The sun dips below the horizon
when I open the door
in my threadbare bathrobe
and watch you shuffle
to a rusty truck that, like us,
has seen far better days.

I'd been hoping you'd leave,
but didn't want to voice it.
I follow your plume of dust
till I cannot see its trail.

Cool comes with the dark,
but both take their time.
From an outdoor bench
I sift through thoughts
of pleasure and inadequacy,
glad for just the company
of tangled cacti and brown terrain,
at home with these
old, worn-out survivors.

There was a time when I downed
endless margaritas, applauding
with the whole patio at a roadside bar
when the sun went down.
Now sunset has crept into my bones.

The porch light has needed
replacing for at least a month,
and I let the dark wrap itself
around me like a woolen blanket.
A howl sounds from the desert,
ominous as the shrouded bottom
of an abandoned mineshaft.

Scott Wiggerman

Affirmation

Artesia, New Mexico

Love, are you sleeping, and how will I
compose the lines that morning invents
again, again familiar? Sunlight curves
along the soft bowls of your breasts,
settles into the folds of our blankets. . . .

For years, I have traced these trails along
arroyos where words for you disappear
within shadows. I have imagined
the surprise soon gone from hands,
abandoned shoulders, your lips

released. Moments contain you
that I may never see—*What is it,*
love? What is it? you ask, waking.
Then *Yes*—assuring me—*Yes, yes love,*
yes. What landscapes have I forgotten?

Steve Wilson

Five Sunday Mornings

Frost thaws,
takes in the morning
sun. For all things,
acceptance.

***

You hedge your bets, awaken
only seconds from the shore.

***

Ravens glide within gray light.
They scree and grraw unearthed, calls
redoubling along the burgeoning
day—an aubade.

***

—milkweed and snakeroot,
blue grama, coneflower—
the grasslands overspread with sky—

***

Unburden. Speak secrets to
the imperturbable dawn.

Steve Wilson

Morning Song for Difficult Times

It was like the night gave me an elixir
to forget the many things there are to be sad about.

Can we not stay here in the shadowed glimpses
of light, divine in the dark, leading with touch and sound?

Why bring the sunrise, rather than stay with the feel
of silk beneath our calves, unweighted feet,

the warmth of one body touching another?
Last night, our son gone at camp, we were loud.

We turned the music on, and we danced in the kitchen,
we drank whiskey and made our way upstairs kissing

and laughing and not caring if the living room blinds
were closed and we became coyotes crying in the hills

with our guilt forgotten for having fun together
without our child. I want you to know,

I have to be able to connect to something else
to survive this time we live in, so when the sun parts

the blinds, I am ready to open my eyes to all it reveals.
Even if I leave you in bed, you helped me remember

I have something to battle for. Yes, our love. Yes,
you. I know that should be enough, but at this point,

I know they don't mean I should fight for myself.
You helped remind me of my body, my voice,

my life. I realize that I cannot allow the sad
to leave me hollow, but must stay right here,

eager for the world I deserve, and for that,
I must fight and enjoy being very alive.

Liza Wolff-Francis

What I learned in heaven

In heaven, there is no darkness
and no one sleeps.

We could do that here too, stay up
all night roaming the streets,

singing drunken songs into the dark,
being the road noise

outside someone's apartment.
We could hold hands and not feel afraid

to skip to the edge of light
where the vast open desert unfolds

a sky much deeper than us, where silence
is like a choir and city sounds

become a distant dream we are inside of.
Forever and infinity is a long time

to not sleep, you say. Let's lie down
and stare up into the spotted darkness

until we feel a part of the earth beneath us
is heaven and dying is trying

to not give in to rest, rather than enjoying
the feel of closing our eyes,

becoming one with the night and finally,
finally, letting sleep come.

Liza Wolff-Francis

Out Here Out of the Weather

How clever we are
        to be
out of the weather.
Look at how we've thought it through.

Cozy. This morning
        it rained
a little.
        It tried to rain
my sad father would say

dribs and drabs
        my mother said
back in Kansas back in the day.

But here on the edge
        of desert
where we don't have many words
for the rain we don't have often

we are grateful for what settles
        the dust
at dawn (madrugada   lovely word!)
the likeliest time for rain.

Jon Kelly Yenser

Hill Country Angelus

A matte of early eventide, timeless, these acres
thumb-printed with sheep and one guard burro
near the fence corner, long lashes unblinking.

Climbing double strands of barbed wire,
she's careful not to snare sweater or jeans,
to leave no threads entwined with wisps of white

already woven into spaced and rusted wire twists.
She wanders this pastoral postcard, seeking prayerful calm
as eight chimes drift over dusky fields from a nearby village.

Disinterested cud-chewers line themselves in parallel
across the expanse, mutton muffs pressed forward,
each balanced on four spindles, rumps to the wind.

Losing track of time, she stretches to visor her view,
singles out Southdowns bunched near northern hills,
prays they'll not face predators overnight.

Clots of clouds spread from roadside to humped horizon.
High fleece above, a mirror of ground below.
Sound barrier breaking, a white scar sears the palette of perfect sky.

Judith Youngers

Evensong

As he was drifting to sleep his thoughts were of horses and of the open country and of horses. Horses still wild on the mesa . . .

~ Cormac McCarthy, *All the Pretty Horses*

Carrying crescendos of color, the sun sets; improbable mists rise. Mysterious notes sweep through measures of drying grama rustling over high-blown prairies. Equine bodies of grace swish through Southwestern mesas. Thin leg spindles attached to muscled flanks bear sculptured torsos that conjure a ballet de corps. All of this in a land not ours to hold. Perhaps you roamed, Equus Caballus, godlike with the Comanche, Ute and Mescalero, gliding through gilt shimmers beneath the dome of chalked sky. We know that you secret ballads under the fringe of your liquid eyes and helix of your ears. You brush the rabbitbrush, snag a carillon of coral bells from waving ocotillo with your flagging tail. Your quarters burnish with shafts of lingering rays that glance off Rincon peaks. We can only question. How do you wedge your thighs through this rugged cordillera? Are you a mirage emerging from desert mesas?

You range untethered, never ours to rein in, even in song. At this day's close, we quiet ourselves with a calming coda. Long into hours of liquid ebony, your neon loins crackle, draw us into rhapsody. Staring into eons of ether, we try to catch stars that staccato over rimmed canyons.

   cleansed with piñon breath
   our voices rise in worship
   you nicker *Amen*

Judith Youngers

Walking at Fort Davis

The roadrunner perches on a sandstone rock
in the broomsedge, expecting
not to be noticed in the golden-brown flame
of grass filled with morning sun. You lead the way
on our sandy mountain trail in a bright blue shirt,
bold as the sky, and I love
you both, for it is early
and the world is a feast
not yet overheated.
I am tasting us,
how we woke
together, as I crouch
in the grass capturing
a photo of the bird,
knowing you will soon disappear
around the craggy bend.

Vanessa Zimmer-Powell

Contributor Notes

Pamela Ahlen (Woodstock, VT) is special events coordinator for Osher Lifelong Learning Institute at Dartmouth. She compiled and edited *Osher's Anthology of Poets and Writers: Celebrating Twenty-Five Years at Dartmouth.* Pamela received an MFA from Vermont College of Fine Arts. She is the author of the chapbook *Gather Every Little Thing* (Finishing Line Press) and the co-author (with Anne Bower) of *Getting it Down on Paper, Shaping a Friendship* (Orchard Street Press).

Luther Allen (Bellingham, WA) was born in New Mexico and lived forty years in the Southwest before moving to the Northwest. He has published two volumes of poetry—*The View from Lummi Island* and *A Spiritual Thread.* His poems appear in numerous journals and anthologies, including *Weaving the Terrain: 100-Word Southwestern Poems* (Dos Gatos Press), *For Love of Orcas, I Sing the Salmon Home, New Mexico Poetry Anthology 2023,* and *The Madrona Project.* Luther views writing as his spiritual practice.

Elizabeth Ambos (Washington, DC) has inhabited multiple careers as a geoscientist, teacher, and administrator in higher education-affiliated organizations. A participant in the PocketMFA program, Ambos is currently working on her MFA in Creative Writing at Hood College. She has published recently in *Cathexis Northwest Press, Wild Roof Journal,* PocketMFA's *RUNNR, Gramercy Review,* and *WWPH Writes.*

Cynthia Anderson (Yucca Valley, CA) has published thirteen poetry collections, most recently *The Far Mountain* (Wise Owl Publications, 2024), *Arrival* (Sheila-Na-Gig Editions, 2023), and *Full Circle* (Cholla Needles Press, 2022). She is co-editor of the anthology *A Bird Black As the Sun: California Poets on Crows & Ravens.* Anderson has lived in California for over forty years.

Conrado Aragón (Los Angeles, CA) grew up in a small border town on the U.S.-Mexico border, where he acquired an abiding fascination with the magic and mystery of the vast deserts of the Southwest. He holds a Master's degree in Romance Languages and Literature (Yale University) and a JD (University of Chicago). Aragón is the author of the novella, *The Phenomenalist.*

Rebecca Aronson (Albuquerque, NM) is the author of three books of poetry, most recently *Anchor,* winner of the Eric Hoffer Award for poetry and the poetry prize from the Philosophical Society of Texas. She has been a recipient of a Yetzirah fellowship, a *Prairie Schooner* Strousse Award, the Loft's Speakeasy Poetry Prize, and a Tennessee Williams Scholarship to Sewanee. Aronson is host of Bad Mouth, a series of words and music.

Cody Baggerly (Ada, OK) is an Oklahoma poet from Chickasaw Country. He has been featured in East Central University's literary journal *Originals, The Rising Phoenix Review,* the Dublin California Poetry Walk, *Wingless Dreamer, Alien Buddha, Literature Today, San Pedro River Review,* and the *NoSleep Podcast.* Baggerly has presented his poetry at the Scissortail Creative Writing Festival and the Woody Guthrie Festival. He is the host of the First Monday Open-Mic held at Kind Origin in Ada.

Virginia Barrett (Lagunitas, CA) earned her MFA in Writing from the University of San Francisco, where she was poetry editor of *Switchback.* Her seventh book of poetry, *The Vessels We Carry Keep Us Alive,* is forthcoming from Saint Julian Press. Her latest editing project, *BLUE: a Hue Are You anthology*, the second volume in a series, was released in April. Barrett has twice received writing residency grants from the Helene Wurlitzer Foundation of Taos, New Mexico.

Patricia Spears Bigelow (San Antonio, TX) has written fiction and poetry about the Southwest. A Pushcart nominee, she has had poetry in newspapers, anthologies and journals, including *Weaving the Terrain: 100-Word Southwestern Poems* and *Bearing the Mask: Southwestern Persona Poems* (Dos Gatos Press); *Is This Forever or What?: Poems and Paintings from Texas; For Every Little Thing: Poems and Prayers to Celebrate the Day;* and her own collection *Midnight Housekeeping* (River Lily Press).

Poet and painter **Elizabeth Black** (Haymarket, VA) lives in the foothills of the Shenandoah Mountains with her husband and ashes of her dog Jack. She finds her muse in nature, inspiring color and movement in paintings, images, and music in poems. Black has published in several national and international journals, including *Blythe Spirit, Hedgerow, First Frost, Northern Virginia Review, Presence, Ribbons,* and several anthologies. She was nominated for a Pushcart Prize in 2024.

Sheila Black (San Antonio, TX) is the author of five poetry collections, most recently a chapbook, *For the Loneliness of Walking Ou*t (Lily Review). Poems and essays have appeared in *Crab Creek Review, The Nation, The New York Times,* and elsewhere. Black is a co-editor of *Beauty is a Verb: The New Poetry of Disability.* She is assistant director of the Virginia G. Piper Center for Creative Writing at Arizona State University.

Gia Bloomstrand (Tucson, AZ) is a queer poet living in the desert of Southern Arizona with her partner. In her early thirties she finally allowed herself the gift of a poetry workshop and has been writing ever since. Her work struggles to capture her deep love for this world and its creatures, humans included, and her anger/fear at what we've destroyed and are destroying. Bloomstrand is new to the submission process but excited to share her writing.

Christine H. Boldt (Aurora, CO), a retired librarian, was a Peace Corps Volunteer in Nigeria in the 1960s and lived in Italy during the 1970s. A resident of Texas since 1981, Boldt recently moved to Colorado. Her collection *Missing, One Muse* won the 2018 Alabama State Poetry Society's Morris Memorial Chapbook Competition. She is the author of *For Every Tatter* (Lamar University Literary Press) and *Minding Her Muse* (forthcoming from the same press).

Sharon V. Brown (Redmond, WA), a retired English professor, writes poetry from the enriched perspective of an older woman, reflecting on loss, change, and fragility. Recent work appears in *Still Point Arts Quarterly, The Lyric, The Senior Class: 100 Poets on Aging, Cirque,* and *Angel City Review.*

Kathleen Burke (Austin, TX) counts place and spirit as favorite subjects. She has created handmade poetry books, including *Haiku Texas*, and enjoys responding to current and collective events on Instagram.

Jeff Burt (Mount Hermon, CA) writes poems that involve mobile expeditions, which become mental and spiritual expeditions as well. He has contributed to *Willows Wept Review, Williwaw Journal, sunlight press,* and others.

Mike Burwell (Arroyo Seco, NM) has published in *Abiko Quarterly, Alaska Quarterly Review, Cloudbank, Poems & Plays,* and *Sin Fronteras.* He is the author of *Cartography of Water* (NorthShore Press) and *Coin on My Tongue*, a semi-finalist for the Tupelo Press Berkshire Prize (2023) and the Black Lawrence Press Hudson Prize (2024).

Tina Carlson (Santa Fe, NM) is the author of three full-length collections of poetry: *Ground, Wind, This Body; We Are Meant to Carry Water,* a collaboration with two other New Mexico poets; and *A Guide to Tongue Tie Surgery,* which received the 2024 New Mexico/Arizona Book Award for Poetry. Carlson has a chapbook, *Obsidian* (Dancing Girl Press). She is an editor of the online journals *Unbroken* and *Hot Flash Literary.*

Nancy Christopherson (Baker City, OR) is the author of *The Leaf.* Her poems have appeared in *Abandon Journal, Aji Magazine, Amethyst Review, Barnstorm Journal, Cirque, Clepsydra Literary Magazine, Common Ground Review, Free State Review, Helen Literary Magazine, Hole In The Head Review, Kosmos Quarterly Spring Gallery of Poets, Moria Literary Magazine, Peregrine, Raven Chronicles, The Cape Rock, The Healing Muse, The Stillwater Review, Third Wednesday, Triggerfish Critical Review, Verseweavers, Willawaw Journal,* and *Xanadu,* among others.

Stan Crawford (Albuquerque, NM) is an attorney and poet living in New Mexico with his wife Dawn and their assorted dogs and cats. His poems have been published in *ABQ inPrint, Borderlands: Texas Poetry Review, The Comstock Review, The Midwest Quarterly, Poet Lore, Water-Stone Review,* and elsewhere. Crawford's poetry collection *Resisting Gravity* (Lamar University Literary Press) was a Finalist for the Best First Book of Poetry Award (Texas Institute of Letters, 2017).

Cheney Crow (Austin, TX) has poems in *The Cortland Review, Tupelo Quarterly, Best of Tupelo Quarterly, International Poetry* (translation), *Terminus* (Poetry@Tech), *The Ekphrastic Review, Scoundrel Time, The Texas Poetry Calendar,* and elsewhere. Her translation of *The Fourth Wall,* a novel by Sorj Chalandon, is forthcoming in spring 2026. Crow earned her MFA in poetry at Warren Wilson College.

Carolyn Dahl (Houston, TX) has poems in *Copper Nickel, Poet Lore, Main Street Rag,* and *The Southern Review,* as well as three chapbooks, and three art books. Dahl's manuscript *A Muddy Kind of Love* won the North Dakota State University chapbook contest and *Art Preserves What Can't Be Saved,* the National Federation of Press Women's chapbook competition. A single poem was the grand prize winner in *ArtLines 2.*

Margo Davis (Houston, TX) wonders which has the greater pull, geographic locale or a pressing need to write. She's enjoyed residencies in the Pacific Northwest, Portugal, Budapest, Spain and Italy. A three-time Pushcart nominee, Davis has poems in *The Ekphrastic Review, Equinox, Passager, Verse Daily, Panoply,* and *Unknotting the Line: The Poetry in Prose* (Dos Gatos Press). Margo is the author of *Quicksilver,* a chapbook. *Uncoupling,* a new collection, is forthcoming from Lamar University Literary Press.

Terry Dawson (Madison, CT) is the author of two poetry collections—*after: poems only a planet could love* (Poets' Choice, 2022) and *Pursuing the Ruin* (Lamar University Literary Press, forthcoming). A retired Presbyterian minister and former adjunct faculty at San Francisco Seminary, Dawson produces the multi-cultural poetry, jazz, and live painting collaborative, Five Voizz Brush, founded in Austin, Texas, where he lived previously and wrote a guest column for the *Austin American-Statesman.*

Marcial Delgado (Albuquerque, NM) is a Chicano poet and filmmaker whose work navigates identity, heritage, and systemic critique. Blending ancestral symbolism with surreal metaphor, their poems explore fate, love, and resistance. Delgado's performance poetry has been featured in slam arenas across the Southwest, and their award-winning short film *Savior*—written and performed by them—examines intergenerational trauma and healing. They are currently experimenting with hybrid forms that fuse spoken word with cinematic and ritual elements.

Mary Margaret Dougherty (George West, TX) writes poetry inspired by Texas, the place and its people, where she has lived all her life. Her poetry has appeared in *The Journal of Undiscovered Poets, Poetry at Round Top, Big Land, Big Sky, Big Hair, Unknotting the Line: The Poetry in Prose* (Dos Gatos Press), *Red River Review, American Cowboy, Rope Burns, English Journal,* and four issues of the *Texas Poetry Calendar.*

Cyra Sweet Dumitru (San Antonio, TX) is one of four certified practitioners of poetic medicine living in Texas. She has published four collections of her poems. Her memoir *Words Make a Way Through Fire: Healing From My Brother's Suicide,* told through prose and poetry, has just been released from She Writes Press with distribution through Simon & Schuster.

Alicia Elkort (Santa Fe, NM) received the Two Sylvias Press Wilder Prize for her second poetry collection, forthcoming in 2026. Her first book, *A Map of Every Undoing* (Stillhouse Press, 2022) won the George Mason University book contest. Elkort is a Pushcart, Best of the Net, and Orison Anthology nominee. Her work appears in numerous journals and anthologies

Kelly Ann Ellis (Houston, TX) has an MA in English from the University of Houston, where she now teaches. She is cofounder of the literary nonprofit hotpoet and managing editor of its online journal *Equinox*. Ellis's poetry explores personal yet universal tensions—between belief and disenchantment, contentment and longing, hope and despair. Her work has been featured in anthologies, film festivals, and even a music and dance production. *The Hungry Ghost Diner* is her first collection (Lamar University Literary Press, 2023).

Nancy Fine (Burns, Oregon) writes fiction, nonfiction, and poetry, sometimes all in the same day. She writes from her wooden desk, pickup-truck desk, a stand-up sort of desk, backpack desk, the truck stop table, and from pieces of paper tucked in her cargo pants' pocket desk. Fine enjoys being in the high desert, where there are more cows than people. Nothing against people, she just prefers plenty of room for them.

Stacey Forbes (Oro Valley, AZ) is the author of the poetry chapbook *Little Thistles* (Finishing Line Press), winner of the 2023 New Women's Voices competition. Her work appears in some of the publications she loves, including *Beloit Poetry Journal, New Ohio Review, Terrain.org,* and *Split Rock Review.* Born in Pennsylvania, Forbes now lives and writes in the fierce and beautiful Sonoran Desert.

Heather D Frankland (Silver City, NM) holds an MFA from New Mexico State University. She was a Peace Corps and Peace Corps Response Volunteer in Peru and Panama. She is the author of a poetry chapbook, *Midwest Musings* (Finishing Line Press). Originally from Indiana, currently Frankland teaches English at Western New Mexico University. She serves as Poet Laureate of Silver City and Grant County.

Belén Thérèse Garza Flores (Mercedes, TX) a Rio Grande Valley writer, explores themes of identity, spirituality, and loss. She has poems in *Gallery Magazine, Odes and Elegies: Eco-Poetry from the Texas Gulf Coast,* and *Boundless 2025.* Influences include Anna Akhmatova, Claribel Alegría, and Francisco Matos Paoli. Garza Flores maintains a blog, *Ojalá Ojalá: Essays From the Valley of Tears*, where she writes about current events and local culture from a mestiza Catholic perspective.

Lenora Rain-Lee Good (Kennewick, WA) is the author of the chapbook *Saying Goodbye to Thomas* (Finishing Line Press, 2025). She writes fiction, radio dramas, and her love—poetry. Good's poetry has appeared in online and print anthologies, including *Quill and Parchment, Fixed and Free,* and *Cirque Journal.* Her favorite poetry quote is by Robert A. Heinlein: "A poet who reads his verse in public may have other nasty habits."

Martha K. Grant (Boerne, TX), a native San Antonian, moved to the Hill Country in 2001 and found in the deep silence of a rural landscape new inspiration for her poetry in a way she rarely did as a city-dweller. From the first appearance of a fox on the feast of St. Mary Magdalene, the resident creatures and critters become soulful muses and sacred emissaries. A poetry MFA at 72 was a natural progression.

Benjamin Green (Jemez Springs, NM) is the author of twelve books, including *His Only Merit* (Finishing Line Press) and the upcoming *Old Man Looking through a Window at Night* (Main Street Rag). At the age of sixty-nine, he hopes his new work articulates a mature vision of the world and does so with some integrity.

Amy L. Greenspan (Austin, TX) is a former managing editor for a legal publishing company. Her poems appear in multiple editions of the *Texas Poetry Calendar* and in collections including *The Senior Class: 100 Poets on Aging, Waco Wordfest Anthology 2023, Texas Poetry Assignment, cattails, Haiku Presence,* and two Dos Gatos Press collections—*Weaving the Terrain: 100-Word Southwestern Poems,* and *Lifting the Sky: Southwestern Haiku and Haiga.*

Ben Griffin (Austin, TX) writes about memory, ruin, and the absurd rituals of being a person. His work blends grief, surrealism, and humor. By day, he works as a copywriter. By night, he writes poems that talk back. A lifetime ago, he discovered poetry under the mentorship of Roger Reeves at the University of Texas at Austin.

Lucy Griffith (Comfort, TX) lives beside the Guadalupe River. As a retired psychologist, she explored the imagined life of the Burro Lady of West Texas in her debut collection, *We Make a Tiny Herd,* earning both the Wrangler and Willa Prizes. Her new collection, *The Place the Spiders Waved,* is a 2025 WILLA Poetry Finalist. Griffith is a Bread Loaf scholar, a Master Naturalist, and is known to stare at the river for long periods of time.

Carol D Guerrero-Murphy (Denver, CO) has a long history of publishing and teaching poetry, including three books—*Tablewalking at Nighthawk,* a finalist for the WILLA Award from Women Writing the West, *Chained Dog Dreams,* and *Bright Path Dark River.* Guerrero-Murphy is a writing coach, editor, fire survivor, professor, and writer with a PhD from Denver University. Publications include *Pilgrimage, Missouri Review, Roanoke Review, Prairie Schooner, Southwest Literary Review, Manifest West, Bronze Bird,* and more.

Sheryl Guterl (Albuquerque, NM) writes from her New Mexico home in the winter and Francestown, New Hampshire in the summer. The dry desert climate, hues of sand and pink, and open skies contrast sharply with the forest damp and green palette of New England, providing inspiration and interest. Guterl has written poetry since her retirement; she finds it both relaxing and challenging. Several poems have been published in periodicals. She is working on a collection.

Ken Hada (Wanette, OK) is the author of twelve collections of poetry, including *Visions for the Night, Come Before Winter,* and *Contour Feathers* (Turning Plow Press, 2025, 2023 and 2021). His work has been honored by The Oklahoma Center for the Book, The Western Writers of America, The National Western Heritage Museum, South Central Modern Language Association, and The Writer's Almanac.

C. T. Holte (Albuquerque, NM) grew up in Minnesota without color TV, played under bridges, along creeks, and in cornfields, and went to many schools. He has had gigs as teacher, peddler, editor, and some less wordy things. Recently, Holte migrated to New Mexico with his partner, the most beautiful girl in the world. He's been published in *Words, Touch, California Quarterly, Months to Years, Mediterranean Poetry, Pensive,* and elsewhere.

Cindy Huyser (Austin, TX) is the author of the full-length poetry collection, *Cartography* (3: A Taos Press, 2025), the contest-winning chapbook *Burning Number Five: Power Plant Poems* (Blue Horse Press 2014), co-author of the collaborative limited-edition chapbook *XIII: Taylor Swift-Inspired Poems* (Float Press, 2025), and co-editor of *Bearing the Mask: Southwestern Persona Poems* (Dos Gatos Press, 2016). She holds an MFA from Pacific University.

D. Iasevoli (Brant Lake, NY) lives in the Adirondacks of New York. He makes bows for archery. Iasevoli has published both essays and poetry, in such titles as *Chiron, American Aesthetic, Albatross, Blue Collar Review, English Journal, The Blue Line Review, Closed Eye Open, Knot, The Fourth River, Words Apart,* and *You Are Here.* His chapbook, *The Less Said,* was featured at the Bowery Poetry Café.

Joy Jacobson (Santa Fe, NM) began her apprenticeship in poetry in the foothills of the Sandia Mountains in the 1990s and continued in New York, where she received an MFA in poetry at the New School. She has had residencies at Vermont Studio Center, MacDowell, Helene Wurlitzer Foundation, and Monson Arts. Currently, Jacobson is working on a series of poems exploring the consequences of drought.

Mark Jodon (Houston, TX) is the author of two full-length books of poetry, *Miles of Silence* (Kelsay Books) and *Day of the Speckled Trout* (Transcendent Zero Press). His poetry has appeared in *Soul by Southwest* and *Pensive: A Global Journal of Spirituality & the Arts.* Jodon recently concluded an unofficial and unauthorized book tour promoting *Miles of Silence* in Scotland.

Kathryn Jones (Walnut Springs, TX) is a poet, journalist, and essayist whose work has appeared in *The New York Times, Texas Monthly,* and numerous literary journals and anthologies. She has a chapbook, *An Orchid's Guide to Life* (Finishing Line Press, 2024), and a full-length collection, *The Solace of Wild Places* (Lamar University Literary Press, 2025). Jones was inducted into the Texas Institute of Letters in 2016.

Kate Kingston (Trinidad, CO) is the author of T*he Future Wears Camouflage* (Middle Creek Publishing, 2025). She is the recipient of the Atlanta Review International Publication Prize, Karen Chamberlain Award, and Ruth Stone Prize, among others. Kingston has received fellowships at the Harwood Museum, Helene Wurlitzer Foundation, Jentel, and Ucross, as well as at Disquiet in Lisbon, Portugal, and Fundación Valparaíso in Mojácar, Spain. Several of her poems have been nominated for a Pushcart Prize.

Sarah Kotchian (Albuquerque, NM) is the author of *Light of Wings* (University of New Mexico Press, 2024), a finalist for the New Mexico/Arizona Book Award in Poetry. Her poetry collection *Camino* received the New Mexico/Arizona Book Award and Seven Sisters Book Award. A contributor at the Bread Loaf Writers' Conference and Pushcart nominee, Kotchian has had work in numerous journals.

Gabrielle Langley (Houston, TX) is the author of *Fairy Tale* (Sable Books, 2023) and *Azaleas on Fire* (Sable Books, 2019). She has won the Lorene Pouncey Poetry Award and the Vivian Nellis Memorial Award for Creative Writing. Langley was also a spearhead and co-editor for the anthology *Red Sky: Poetry on the global epidemic of violence against women* (Sable Books, 2016).

Gayle Lauradunn (Albuquerque, NM) is the author of *Consider This,* new in 2025. Nature and history are two themes that run through her work. *Reaching for Air* was named Finalist for Best First Book of Poetry (Texas Institute of Letters). *All the Wild and Holy: A Life of Eunice Williams, 1696-1785,* received the National Poetry Book Award (North Street). Lauradunn's third book is *The Geography of Absence.* Many poems have appeared in journals and anthologies.

Eileen Lawrence (Round Rock, TX) is the author of a chapbook, *How to Escape a Burning House* (Finishing Line Press, 2025). Her poetry has been published by Dos Gatos Press, Mutabilis Press, the Fargo Public Library, Visions International, *Equinox Journal, Kindred Characters, The Ekphrastic Review,* and *formidable woman sanctuary*.

Suzanne Lee (Littleton, CO) is a historian and writer. Growing up in the small towns of Arizona and New Mexico, she developed a love of the landscapes, spirit, and people of the Southwest. Her poetry has appeared in *Sow's Ear, Snowy Egret,* and *Colorado Life*. Her nonfiction credits include investigative reports and articles in military history.

Writer, editor, and teacher **Wayne Lee** (Santa Fe, NM) has poems in *Slipstream, The New Guard, Writer's Digest,* and other journals and anthologies. Recipient of the 2012 Fischer Prize, he has been nominated for a Pushcart Prize and four Best of the Net Awards. Lee's collection *Dining on Salt: Four Seasons of Septets* is new from Cornerstone Press.

John Macker (Santa Fe, NM) has lived in northern New Mexico for over thirty years. His most recent poetry books are *The Blues Drink Your Dreams Away: Selected Poems, 1983-2018; Atlas of Wolves;* and *Belated Mornings*. Macker's 2020 book, *Desert Threnody,* essays and short fiction, received the 2021 New Mexico/Arizona Book Award. His full-length play, *Death of El Chapultepec Bar,* was produced by Teatro Paraguas in Santa Fe in October, 2025.

Bram MacLihr (Albuquerque, NM) is a former linguistics professor. He has performed poetry in Albuquerque in many venues, as well as the Winter Solstice Poetry Reading in Placitas, New Mexico. MacLihr's poetry explores nature and queer identity among other themes. He can often be found hiking in the Sandias, camping in the Jemez, or playing tug-of-war with the dog.

Gordon Magill (Tallahassee, FL) has taught writing in public schools and at the Institute of American Indian Arts in Santa Fe. He has written many interpretive exhibits with Discovery Exhibits of Santa Fe. Magill has published articles and poetry in magazines and anthologies, including *Echoes of the Cordillera* (Museum of the Big Bend, Alpine, Texas) and *Weaving the Terrain: 100-Word Southwestern Poems* (Dos Gatos Press).

Jonathan Mahaffie (Federal Way, WA) was recently selected as 2025 Lakewold Gardens Poet, where his poem "Bamboo" was featured in Poetry in the Gardens. He is a pediatric speech language pathologist in the Pacific Northwest, where he writes about newfound fatherhood, his obsession with the blackberry, and inequities in the public schooling system.

Dawn Manning (Oley, PA) resides in the former tollhouse of a covered bridge, where she writes, consults, and metalsmiths. Manning is the author of *Postcards from the Dead Letter Office* (Burlesque Press). Honors for her work include the Gylys Villanelle Prize, Hugh J. Luke Award, and the Beullah Rose Poetry Prize, among others. Her poems have appeared in *32 Poems, Ecotone, Pleiades, Prairie Schooner, Verse Daily,* and other literary journals.

Linda Maxwell (Georgetown, SC) grew up in New Mexico's Valencia County and graduated from the University of New Mexico. She currently teaches high school in South Carolina, where she has freelanced for *The Georgetown Times*. Her poetry has appeared in *The Chaffin Journal, Southern Women's Review,* and *Weaving the Terrain: 100-Word Southwestern Poems* (Dos Gatos Press).

Bray McDonald (Rio Rancho, NM) finished a triple major degree in Environmental Issues from the University of South Alabama in 2000, where he studied poetry under Sue Brannan Walker and Walt Darring. He retired as Senior Educator at the Tennessee Aquarium and moved to Rio Rancho, where he spends the majority of his time focused on writing. McDonald has been published in numerous journals in the U. S., Canada, and Europe.

Michael McIrvin (Cheyenne, WY) is the author of several poetry collections, including *Optimism Blues: Poems Selected and New* (2003) and *Hearing Voices* (Fearful Symmetry, 2020). His most recent novel is *The Blue Man Dreams the End of Time* (2009). McIrvin lives on the High Plains of Wyoming.

John Milkereit (Houston, TX), a mechanical engineer, has completed an MFA in Creative Writing at the Rainier Writing Workshop. His work has appeared in various literary journals such as *The Comstock Review, San Pedro River Review,* and previous issues of the Dos Gatos Press series, Poetry of the Southwestern U.S. Milkereit's fifth full-length collection of poems is forthcoming from Kelsay Books.

Michele M Miller (Tucson, AZ) holds an MFA in creative writing from the University of Arizona. Honors for her poetry include an Arizona Commission on the Arts fellowship, as well as runner-up designation for the National Poetry Series and the Kore Press First Book Prize. Her chapbook *The Pocket Museum of Natural History* is newly published as a finalist in the New Women's Voices Series from Finishing Line Press. Miller's poems have appeared in various journals and have been short-listed for international competitions.

Judith Austin Mills (Pflugerville, TX) writes poetry and fiction. Her sequence of poems *Accidental Joy* is a Plain View Press publication, as are her Texas Revolution novels. *The Dove Shall Fly* won a Will Rogers Medallion. Her short stories have appeared in literary journals, including *The Nebraska Review* and *Analecta*. The *Texas Poetry Calendar* has included her work.

Penelope Moffet (Culver City, CA) is the author of three chapbooks, most recently *Cauldron of Hisses* (Arroyo Seco Press, 2022). Her poems appear in *Calyx, Eclectica, ONE ART* and other literary journals. A full-length collection of her poetry will be published by Sheila-Na-Gig Editions in 2026.

Gayle Moran (Houston, TX) has dabbled in writing activities off and on for much of her life. She has short stories and poems in a variety of publications, and she wrote a novel for her doctoral dissertation. Most recently, Moran has published poems in *The Ekphrastic Review, MockingHeart Review,* and *Unknotting the Line: The Poetry in Prose* (Dos Gatos Press). She recently retired from teaching communication skills to engineering students at Rice University.

karla k. morton (Raton, NM)) has seventeen books, with work published in journals such as *American Life in Poetry, Alaska Quarterly Review, Southword, Arkansas Review, descant, Boulevard, Comstock Review, Atlanta Review, Lascaux Review, Grub Street, New Ohio Review,* and *The Southern Review.* Morton has won a National Heritage Wrangler Award, Spur Award, and Foreword Indies National Book Award. She was the 2010 Texas State Poet Laureate and has been a nominee for the National Cowgirl Hall of Fame.

Ruth Mota (Watsonville, CA) is a poet in the Santa Cruz Mountains of California who travels frequently to New Mexico. Over fifty of her poems have been published in online and print journals, including *The Atlanta Review, Gyroscope Review,* and *Fourth River.* Mota's chapbook, *Kitchen Table Midwife of the Dispossessed,* is forthcoming from Finishing Line Press.

Jules Nyquist (Placitas, NM) is the founder of Jules' Poetry Playhouse. Her recent award-winning books are *Atomic Paradise, Homesick, then,* and *The Sestina Playbook* (Poetry Playhouse Publications). She earned her PhD in Post-Secondary Adult Education from Capella University and her MFA in Writing and Literature from Bennington College. Nyquist teaches classes, curates events, and presents at conferences.

Katherine Durham Oldmixon Garza (Austin, TX) is the author of *Life Afterlife / A Book of the Hours* (3: A Taos Press, 2024) and the chapbook *Water Signs* (Finishing Line Press, 2009). She directs the Poetry at Round Top Festival held annually in Round Top, Texas. Now professor emerita (i.e., retired from university life), Dr. Kat is a full-time writer, ecological gardener, and visual artist.

Jeremy Paden (Lexington, KY) is a poet, translator, and Professor of Latin American Literature at Transylvania University. He served as the spring 2025 guest poetry editor for a special volume of the *Southern Humanities Review* on Appalachian poetry. *Tupelo Quarterly 35* included a selection of sixteen Latin American poets Paden curated and translated. His recent books include *how to recognize god's chosen* (Accents Publishing, 2025) and his translation of Mario Meléndez's *Waiting for Perec* (Action, Spectacle, 2025).

Misha Penton (Houston, TX) is a multidisciplinary artist whose work spans music, performance, video, poetry, and prose. Her work draws from the dreamscape of myth and imagination; her texts often become lyrics and libretti for her own vocal compositions and collaborations. Penton's writing has appeared in *The Future Fire, The Wild Word, Corvid Queen, About Place Journal,* and *Abyss & Apex Magazine*. Her poem "Under the Boards" was a 2020 Pushcart Prize nominee.

Jennifer Frank Pontzer (Albuquerque, NM) writes to discover the universal in the specific. Living in New Mexico and working as a sustainability practitioner inform and inspire many of the themes in her poetry. Pontzer's poems have appeared in journals and anthologies such as *Kalliope, Phoebe, Harwood Anthology, Looking Back to Place, Adobe Walls,* and *Central Avenue Then & Now*. With roots in Pittsburgh and Washington, DC, she has called Albuquerque home for nearly thirty years.

Frank Pool (Austin, TX), a long-time educator and columnist, has been writing poetry for many years. He has been published in such journals as *Borderlands, di-verse-city, Sulphur River Review, Ocotillo Review, Equinox,* and *Best Texas Writing II*. He is the author of *Depth of Field* (2001). For five years Pool chaired the board of the Austin International Poetry Festival; he edited the *Austin Younger Poets Award Anthology* for student writers.

Vince Puzick (Colorado Springs, CO) writes poems and essays that explore humans' relationships with the environment, as well as fly fishing, recovery, and family. While he mostly writes nonfiction essays, Puzick likes to explore the intersection of poetry and prose, the lyric essay and the prose poem. He recently published a memoir, *In the Middle of Things*, about forgiveness, his relationship with his father, and self-image.

David Radavich (Charlotte, NC) writes poetry, drama, and essays. His plays have been performed across the U.S. and in Europe. His latest books are *Unter der Sonne / Under the Sun: German Poems* (Deutscher Lyrik, 2021) and *Here's Plenty* (Cervena Barva, 2023). Born in Boston and raised in Idaho, Radavich currently lives in North Carolina.

Morgan Ray (Salt Lake City, UT) gave up filmmaking and cataloguing dinosaur bones to write poetry. Her work has appeared in *The Ekphrastic Review, Unknotting the Line: The Poetry in Prose* (Dos Gatos Press), *Unbroken Journal, Gigantic Sequins,* and *Contemporary Haibun Online*. Ray was nominated for the 2023 Best of the Net Literary Awards; her work is included in *The Ekphrastic Review's* 2024 anthology, *The Memory Palace*.

Erica Reid (Fort Collins, CO) is the author of *Ghost Man on Second* (Autumn House Press, 2024), winner of the Donald Justice Poetry Prize. Reid serves as Poetry Faculty within Western Colorado University's MFA program.

Sharon Rhutasel Jones (Los Ranchos, NM) is the author of *Counting the Ways* (Kelsay Books, 2025). She wrote about her fifty-two years of teaching in *Living by Ear: Memoir of a Wayward Teacher*. Her longer poems are published in various anthologies, including *Poets of the Southwest* and two Dos Gatos Press collections—*Bearing the Mask: Southwestern Persona Poems*, and *Weaving the Terrain: 100-Word Southwestern Poems*. Her haiku appear in journals including *Modern Haiku, Frogpond, Prune Juice,* and *Hedgerow*.

John Roche (Placitas, NM) first fell under New Mexico's spell as a teenager in the 1970s. Decades later he met his future wife Jules Nyquist at a poetry conference in Albuquerque. Together, they run Jules' Poetry Playhouse. Roche's most recent books are *Joe Rides Again* (FootHills Publishing) and *Tubbables* (Poetry Playhouse Publications).

Barbara Rockman (Santa Fe, NM) is the author of *Sting and Nest,* winner of the New Mexico/Arizona Book Award, and *to cleave,* recipient of the National Press Women Book Prize. For twenty-eight years, she led poetry workshops at Santa Fe Community College, Esperanza Shelter for Battered Families, and in community workshops. Co-curator of Poets@HERE reading series, Rockman is a member of the Voice Project, bringing poetry to unhoused communities. A new collection, *Night said*, is forthcoming in 2026 from University of New Mexico Press

Aroma Rodrigues (Bellevue, WA) is a poet who explores perception, travel, and the intersections of culture and language. Her poems draw from lived cross-cultural experiences and an interest in how communication shapes identity. Rodrigues has read and spoken internationally; her writing reflects a curiosity about history, place, and belonging. She lives between worlds of observation and imagination, creating poetry that bridges geography and human connection.

Gary S. Rosin (Mountain View, CA) has work in *Cold Moon Journal, MacQueen's Quinterly, The Ekphrastic Review, Texas Poetry Assignment, The Senior Class* (Lamar University Literary Press), *Verse Virtual,* and elsewhere. He has been nominated for a Pushcart Prize and Best of the Net. Rosin has two chapbooks, *Standing Inside the Web* (Bear House Publishing, 1990), and *Fire and Shadows* (Legal Studies Forum, 2008). He is a Contributing Editor of *MacQueen's Quinterly.*

Shelli Rottschafer (Louisville, CO) has a doctorate from the University of New Mexico, Albuquerque (2005) in Latin American Contemporary Literature. From 2006 to 2023 Shelli was a Spanish professor at a small liberal arts college in Michigan. She holds an MFA in Creative Writing with a concentration in Poetry from Western Colorado University, Gunnison (2025). Rottschafer lives and writes in Colorado and New Mexico with her partner and their rescue pup.

Janet Ruth (Corrales, NM) is an ornithologist and poet. Her writing focuses on connections to the natural world, from dawn to dusk. Recent poems appeared in *The Nature of Our Times, The Ekphrastic Review,* and multiple anthologies. Her sonnet, "A World That Shimmers," winner of the True Concord Poetry Contest, was set to music and performed by True Concord Voices and Orchestra in 2023. Ruth's collection *Feathered Dreams* was a Finalist for the 2018 New Mexico/Arizona Book Awards.

Steven Schroeder (Chicago, IL) is a poet and visual artist who lives and works in Chicago. Born in north central Texas, he grew up on the high plains in the Texas Panhandle. Schroeder has been painting and writing poetry for sixty years and has called Chicago home for fifty.

Katherine DiBella Seluja (Santa Fe, NM) is a poet and microfiction writer. She is the author of three poetry collections, most recently *Point of Entry* (University of New Mexico Press, 2023). Seluja's poem "November Fruit" is part of the Taos Poetry in Nature project and is on permanent display at the Helene Wurlitzer Foundation in Taos. Her chapbook, *New World Apothecary,* is forthcoming from Ambidextrous Bloodhound Press. Katherine is a poetry editor at *Unbroken Journal.*

Audell Shelburne (Tahlequah, OK) has published poems in various journals and anthologies, including those by Dos Gatos Press, as well as *descant, Borderlands: Texas Poetry Review, di-verse-city, Loud Coffee, Verse Virtual,* and others. He is currently Dean of the College of Liberal Arts at Northeastern State University in Tahlequah, Oklahoma, where he has previously taught poetry and other courses in literature since 2011. Shelburne enjoys spending time with his wife and children, pretending to cook, and dabbling in watercolors.

Rebecca A Spears (Nacogdoches, TX), author of *Brook the Divide* and *The Bright Obvious,* has poems, essays, and reviews in *TriQuarterly, Narrative, Barrow Street, Verse Daily,* and other publications. *Brook the Divide* was shortlisted for Best First Book of Poetry (Texas Institute of Letters 2020). Most recently, Spears has been awarded a Poetry Fellowship from Porches Writing Retreat (2024) and named Writer-in-Residence at Dairy Hollow House (2025). In March 2025, she received the *Equinox* Prose Award.

Victoria Stefani (Tucson, AZ) lives, writes, and paints in the Arizona desert. Her work has appeared in journals including *The North American Review,* as well as *Weaving the Terrain: 100-Word Southwestern Poems* (Dos Gatos Press). A student of literature, folklore, and mythology, Stefani has taught literature and writing at Humboldt State University and the University of Arizona.

Prosser Stirling (Washington, DC) is a National Federation of State Poetry Societies multiple award-winning poet. His most recent collection is *Somewhere, in front of my name* (Saint Julian Press). A Native of Galveston, Texas, Stirling is a member of the Poetry Society of Texas.

Sharon Suzuki-Martinez (Tempe, AZ) won the Washington Prize for her latest book, *The Loneliest Whale Blues* (The Word Works), and the MVP Prize for her first book, *The Way of All Flux* (New Rivers Press). Her micro-chapbook is *A Glimpse of Birds over O'odham Land* (Rinky Dink Press). She lives on the homeland of the Akimel O'odham.

Larry D. Thomas (Las Cruces, NM), 2008 Texas Poet Laureate, is a member of the Texas Institute of Letters. Since November 2024, he has published a poetry chapbook, *Letting the Light Work: Poems of Mexico,* and three poetry pamphlets with *OPEN: Journal of Arts & Letters,* the most recent of which is *Musing the Crossroads: Poems of the Mississippi River Delta* (Hot Button Press imprint). Thomas lives in the Chihuahuan Desert of southwestern New Mexico.

Shelby Tuthill (Portland, OR) is a queer writer and psychologist. Her work has appeared in *Human Parts, The Golden Key,* and *Funicular Magazine.*

Ron Wallace (Durant, OK) is an Oklahoma native and currently an adjunct instructor of Literature, Composition, and Fiction Writing at Southeastern Oklahoma State University in Durant. He is the author of eleven books of poetry, five of which have been finalists in the Oklahoma Book Awards, with *Renegade and Other Poems* winning the 2018 Award. A multiple Pushcart Prize nominee, Wallace has recently been published in *Oklahoma Today, Oklahoma Humanities Magazine, Emerge Magazine,* and a number of other magazines and journals.

Lynda Gerdin Webb (Leander, TX) has an MA from the University of Texas at El Paso, where she studied fiction with Raymond Carver. Her fiction and poetry have been published by *About Place Journal, Flora Fiction, Persimmon Tree, SouthShore Review, Big Bend Literary Magazine,* Beach Chair Press, and Central Texas Writer's Society.

Marilyn Westfall (Lubbock, TX) holds a PhD in literature and creative writing from Texas Tech University. Her poetry is featured in earlier Dos Gatos Press anthologies, as well as *Enchantment of the Ordinary* (Mutabilis Press), *The Southern Poetry Anthology, Volume VIII: Texas* (Texas Review Press), and *Echoes of the Cordillera* (Museum of the Big Bend). Westfall chairs her local writers' group.

Janice Whittington (Lubbock, TX) is the author of the poetry chapbook *Does My Father Dream of Sons?* (University of West Florida), as well as *Into a Thousand Mouths,* a Walt McDonald Series Winner from Texas Tech University Press. Whittington has poems in *The Beloit Poetry Journal, Touchstone, Mississippi Valley Review, Kansas Quarterly, Writer's Forum,* and *Southern Poetry Review,* as well as two Dos Gatos Press anthologies—*Weaving the Terrain: 100-Word Southwestern Poems* and *Unknotting the Line: The Poetry in Prose.*

Steve Wilson (San Marcos, TX) has poems in journals and anthologies nationwide, as well as in six collections, the most recent entitled *Complicity* (2023).

Liza Wolff-Francis (Carrboro, NC) holds an MFA in Creative Writing from Goddard College. She wrote the play *Border Rising,* performed in Albuquerque and Silver City, New Mexico, as well as Tucson, Arizona. A feminist ecopoet, Wolff-Francis has taught creative writing workshops for over a decade. Her writing is widely published. Her poetry chapbook is *Language of Crossing,* about the Mexico-U.S. border; her full-length collection is *48 hours down the shore* (Kelsay Books, 2024).

Jon Kelly Yenser (Albuquerque, NM) was born and raised and educated in Kansas. He had several jobs—from copy-editing to fund-raising—before retiring to Albuquerque, where he lives with his wife, Pamela Yenser, a memoirist and poet. Yenser has published two collections in the Mary Burritt Christiansen Poetry Series from University of New Mexico Press.

Following decades of educational writing, **Judith Youngers** (Comfort, TX) now focuses on poetry. As she experiments with form, Youngers writes primarily narrative poetry of place and witness. In addition to a chapbook, *Chameleon in Word Clothing,* she is published in juried collections, including *Avocet Quarterly, Through Layered Limestone,* and *Echoes of the Cordillera.* In the village of Comfort, she and a writing cohort host a popular live quarterly reading of recognized poets.

Vanessa Zimmer-Powell (Landrum, SC) has had poetry on the radio, in numerous journals and anthologies; she has received awards and honors for her work. Zimmer-Powell has a chapbook, *Woman Looks into an Eye* (Dancing Girl Press). She was a finalist in the 2024 Mutabilis Press chapbook competition. Her cinepoems have been shown at Gulf Coast Film Festival, ReelPoetry Film Festival, and the Copenhagen Nature & Culture International Film Festival.

The Editors

A Pushcart honoree with a personal essay in *Pushcart Prize XLII,* **David Meischen** is the author of *Nopalito, Texas: Stories* (University of New Mexico Press, 2024) and *Caliche Road Poems* (Lamar University Press ,2024). *Anyone's Son,* from 3: A Taos Press, was honored with Best First Book of Poetry from the Texas Institute of Letters (2020). Meischen's work has appeared in *The Common, Copper Nickel, The Gettysburg Review, Naugatuck River Review, The San Pedro River Review, ,* and elsewhere. A former juror for the Kimmel Harding Nelson Center for the Arts, he is an alumnus of the Jentel Arts residency program. Co-founder and Managing Editor of Dos Gatos Press, he lives on Albuquerque's West Mesa with his husband—also his co-publisher and co-editor—Scott Wiggerman.

Widely published in journals and anthologies—many in poetic form—**Scott Wiggerman** is the author of four books of poetry—*Beginning and Ending with Emily: Ghazals & Golden Shovels* (Casa Urraca Press, forthcoming, 2026), *Leaf and Beak: Sonnets, Presence,* and *Vegetables and Other Relationships.* Co-founder of Dos Gatos Press and founding editor of the Press series, Poetry of The Southwestern U.S., Wiggerman has edited numerous poetry publications, including best-selling craft books *Wingbeats I & II: Exercises & Practice in Poetry.* A member of the Texas Institute of Letters, he lives with his husband, the writer David Meischen, in the shadow of Albuquerque's Three Sisters volcanos.